Th

HIDDEN

of the

CHANNEL ISLANDS

Jersey, Guernsey, Alderney, Sark & Herm

Edited by
Joanna Billing

Published by:
Travel Publishing Ltd
7a Apollo House, Calleva Park
Aldermaston, Berks, RG7 8TN

ISBN 1 90124 115 7

OTHER TITLES IN THE HIDDEN PLACES SERIES

Devon & Cornwall
Dorset, Hants & Isle of Wight
East Anglia
Heart of England
Lancashire & Cheshire
Lake District & Cumbria
North Wales
Northumberland & Durham
Somerset, Avon. Glocs & Wilts
South East
South Wales
Thames & Chilterns
Welsh Borders
Yorkshire & Humberside

England
Ireland
Scotland
Wales

Typesetting by: J Billing, Great Sutton, South Wirral
Printing by: Nuffield Press, Abingdon
Cartography by: Oxford Cartographers

Line Drawings: Sarah Bird

Editor: Joanna Billing

Cover photograph: Tony Reading

Tony lives in Jersey but works principally abroad as Art Director on such feature films as the James Bond "Tomorrow Never Dies". In his infrequent spare time he paints local watercolours and house portraits exclusively for CABBAGES & KINGS in St Helier. The shop also commissioned a series of Jersey Limited Edition prints, and a section of "Gorey" is shown on the front cover.

Foreword

THE HIDDEN PLACES is designed to be an easy to use guide, taking you, in this instance, on a gentle tour through the beautiful countryside of the Channel Islands. However, our books cover many areas and now encompass most of the British Isles. We have combined interesting descriptions of the well-known and enduring tourist attractions with those more secluded and as yet little known venues, easy to miss unless you know exactly where you are going.

We include hotels, inns, restaurants, tea shops, various types of accommodation, historic houses, museums, gardens, craft centres and general attractions throughout these fascinating islands, together with our research on local history. Most places have a line drawing and a brief description of the services offered. Maps for each chapter can be found at the back of the book.

We do not include firm prices or award merits. We merely wish to point you to *The Hidden Places* which will hopefully improve your enjoyment of a holiday or business trip and tempt you to return. The places featured in this book will, we are sure, be pleased if you mention that it was *The Hidden Places* that prompted you to visit.

THE HIDDEN PLACES OF THE CHANNEL ISLANDS

CONTENTS

CHAPTER ONE
JERSEY

Le Moulin de Quétivel

1
JERSEY

Introduction

Jersey is the largest (9 miles long and 5 miles wide) and wealthiest of the Channel Islands, it is also only some 17 miles from the French coast. Jersey is probably best known, as is Guernsey, as a tax haven and financial centre and, indeed, income tax here is very low, there is no VAT and over 50 major finance companies and banks have their base here. But there is a lot more to Jersey and, whilst there is certainly a lot of money here, there is also a wealth of history, quiet country lanes, secluded sandy beaches, glorious weather and, of course, masses of flowers and the world famous Jersey Zoo.

Though Jersey is a dependency of the Crown, it is not a dependency of Parliament; it is self-governing and the Island is not represented in Westminster. This self-governing status dates back to the time before 1204 when the whole of the Channel Islands were part of Normandy and they have never been incorporated into the United Kingdom. In practice, this is what gives Jersey its own responsibility for fiscal affairs and also its independent judicial system. The governing body, the States, is composed of three bodies; 12 Senators, 12 Constables and 29 Deputies, headed by the President who is also the Chief Magistrate in the Royal Court on the Island. Though the States controls the Island's internal affairs new laws must be ratified by Her Majesty.

Divided into 12 parishes, each with a parish church, the Island is well laid out and, despite the large buildings and intense cultivation, there is more open land here than on any other of the islands. The great tidal range, which is common to most of the islands, exposes some 12 square miles of sand and rock pools along the southeast coast whilst the steep cliffs of the north coast provide some spectacular views.

The Queen of the Channel, Jersey, today manages to combine a flourishing tourist industry with its more traditional farming economy. The Island's Jersey Cow is known throughout the world, not only for its long black eyelashes and short dished face, but also for its high fat content milk. Smaller than most breeds, Jersey cows on a modest food intake can produce a high yield and this has ensured the breed's survival. The purity of the herds on the Island is closely guarded and they have been isolated here since 1789 though many cattle have been exported over the years and there are large herds in both the United States and New Zealand.

Famous for the Jersey Royal potato, a particularly delicious early potato traditionally served on its own with salt, butter, black pepper and fresh mint, many fields on the Island are also given over to growing flowers that are flown around the world. The mild climate, aided by the Gulf Stream, guards against frosts and spring comes early to add great splashes of colour to the luscious green landscape of inland Jersey. The success of this horticultural industry is celebrate by a series of festivals held in August. Known as the Battle of the Flowers, today they are peaceful affairs with processions of flower-bedecked floats. In years gone by the strength of the design and construction of the floats was tested when people swarmed all over them, grabbing handfuls of flowers and throwing them at each other.

Finally, Jersey black butter is not quite what it seems, like so many things on the Island. Also known as du nier beurre, it is in fact made from a mixture of apples, sugar, liquorice and a variety of spices all heated together for about 24 hours in new cider. Sweet and syrupy, it is traditionally served spread on toast or gâche (a tasty Island sweetmeat).

The West

ST HELIER

The capital of Jersey, the town is named after a 6th century Belgian monk who settled on the islet out in the bay that is now occupied by Elizabeth Castle. Living as a hermit, St Helier was beheaded by a band of passing pirates and his death is commemorated in the parish coat of arms by two crossed axes.

Originally marshland, Le Marais de St Helier, the fishing hamlet grew up around the **Parish Church** which was probably built during the 11th century. There have been many additions and alterations to the Town

Church, as it is known, over the centuries, notably the roof which was raised in the 14th century when the small old Norman windows were also replaced by large ones with elaborate tracery. The nave was not extended until 1804. The oldest memorial in the Church is to Maximilian Norreys, who died of his wounds whilst fighting in France in 1591. The courage of Major Francis Peirson, the hero of the Battle of Jersey in 1781, is commemorated by a memorial tablet and a granite slab under the crossing.

For centuries **Royal Square** was the market place until the Market Hall opened in 1880. As well as being the centre for the Island's trade, it was also the site of public punishments; two witches were executed here in 1648 and their bodies burned and, as late as 1835, three Jews were exposed in the pillory for forgery. There were also the parish stocks and, in 1619, Katherine Le Sauteur was ordered to sit in them, with her riding breeches by her side, for joining in revelry by dressing up as a man and wearing breeches. It was also in this Square that Charles II, staying on the Island for a short period after his father's execution, was crowned king. It was not for another decade that he was crowned King in Britain.

The Square was also the site of the Battle of Jersey which took place on the morning of January 6, 1781. A French soldier of fortune, Philippe Charles Félix Macquart, secretly landed on the Island with 600 troops and made for Royal Square. The then Lieutenant-Governor, thinking the force to be greater than it actually was, ordered a surrender but neither the British garrison nor the Jersey Militia agreed. Captain Mulcaster, based at Elizabeth Castle, refused to surrender, saying that he did not understand French, whilst Major Francis Peirson rushed to the town with all available troops. The ensuing battle left Macquart dead and the brave young Major mortally wounded. A granite slab marks the place where he fell and he is still remembered as the Island's most popular hero.

The **Statue of George II**, erected in 1751, commemorates the fact that he was the last monarch to lead his troops in battle (at Dettingen in 1743). It is also a mark of appreciation of the King's gift of £200 to the Jersey States to enable them to continue the building of the harbour which commenced in 1700. The monarch is dressed as a Roman Emperor with a laurel crown on his head and it is from this statue that all distances in the Island are measured.

The Island's parliament, one of the oldest assemblies in the Commonwealth, is housed in the **States Chamber**. The present building was

Liberation Sculpture, St Helier

erected in 1887 and, before this, the States used a room above the Court House. Inside, three horse-shoe tiers face the dais on which sits the Bailiff and the Lieutenant-Governor; the Senators sit on their left and the Constables and Deputies of the Parishes in the centre and on their right. Charles II presented the Island's parliament with the silver gilt mace for the loyalty and hospitality he received during his time here. Visitors can listen to debates (on Tuesdays when parliament is in session) from the Public Gallery.

Before the construction of the **Town Hall**, in 1871, parish meetings had been held in the Church of St Helier and also in some of the principal hotels. The Town Hall has a collection of paintings which includes works by Le Capelain and Ouless, two local artists of the 19th century.

Founded by Phillipe Falle, the **Public Library** outgrew its first building and was housed in a purpose built section of the States Building in 1886. Around the interior dome can be seen the names of three distinguishing Jerseymen other than Falle; Le Quesne and Durrell who were both historians and Wace, Jersey's first poet. The new library building was opened in Halkett Place in 1990.

The traditions, culture and history of Jersey can be seen at the **Jersey Museum**, which opened in 1992. There is a recreation of the 250,000 year old La Cotte archeological site and the latest 20th century computer technology is used to bring to life the numerous displays at this award winning museum. It is open daily all year round but closed from 1 pm on Sundays. Life on the Island during the Second World War was a dramatic contrast to the peace and success seen here today. The **Island Fortress Museum** gives today's visitors an insight into the terrible and uncertain days of the five years of German occupation. The exhibits include two field kitchens retrieved from wartime tunnels and the original surrender demand documents. Housed in a converted 19th century warehouse on New North Quay, the **Occupation Tapestry Gallery** displays the 12 tapestries, stitched by the people of Jersey in the largest community project ever, telling of the life of the Island under occupation.

Liberation Square was created in 1945 to commemorate the end of the German Occupation. At the centre of the attractive plaza is a sculpture by Philip Jackson; a bronze statue of flag-waving Jerseymen and women. Once controversial, the sculpture is fast becoming one of St Helier's major landmarks.

The Island established its own postal administration in 1969 and Jersey stamps have gained an international reputation for the excellence of the design and the overall presentation of the stamps. Always popular with visitors, there are five or six new issues of stamps every year, usually commemorating special anniversaries and events. The **Jersey Philatelic Bureau**, in the main Post Office, is open daily Monday to Friday and until noon on Saturday.

Overlooking St Helier from a hill once known as La Montagne de la Ville (Town Hill) **Fort Regent** was always thought to have military significance. In 1551 Sir Edward Seymour, the Island's Governor and brother-in-law to Henry VIII, first sought to build a fort here but, when sinking a well was too difficult, the idea was abandoned. It was not until after the Battle of Jersey, in 1781, that the plan was put into operation and General Don laid the foundations of the Fort. It was named after the Prince Regent, who became George IV. The Fort's guns were never used in hostile action but when the Germans invaded in 1940 they fortified Fort Regent and placed heavy guns here to fire at passing British aircraft. It is now a leisure centre and a key tourist attraction with entertainment and sporting facilities.

The first harbour at St Helier was begun 1700 and was a long time in completion. It also proved to be very inconvenient as ships could only enter and leave the harbour during appropriate states of the tide. To remedy this the north pier was begun in 1770 and south pier completed in 1822. As trade increased greatly, particularly with Newfoundland, a larger harbour was needed and the outer harbour was begun in 1841 and completed in 1846. Albert Pier was named after the Prince Consort who laid the foundation stone in 1847 and the newest part of the harbour was opened by Queen Elizabeth II during her visit here in 1989.

On the rocky islet in St Aubin's Bay, once the home of the hermit, St Helier, an Abbey was built in 1155. Although the Abbey was demoted to a Priory in 1179, it survived until the Reformation in the late 1530s. In the 1590s, the Island's Governor, Sir Walter Raleigh, built **Elizabeth Castle** on the priory site and this superseded Mont Orgueil as the Island's chief defensive position. During his brief stay on Jersey, between 1649 and 1650, Charles II held his court at the Castle and it is also doubtful that he stayed in any of the grand houses on the Island. Reached by foot at low tide along a causeway from St Helier, Elizabeth Castle is open to the public daily between March and October and houses three exhibitions; in particular, there is one on the life of the soldiers who have been billeted on the Island over the centuries.

Jersey is Britain's most southerly resort and the mild climate enables the visitor to holiday out of season and at **The Stafford Hotel**, you will find an excellent reduced tariff, allowing you to save money whilst still enjoying everything that the Island has to offer. The Hotel is conveniently situated right in the very heart of St Helier, Jersey's main shopping centre and capital parish. The shops, where goods can be purchased free of VAT, are within easy walking distance of the Hotel, as is the beautiful beach of St Aubin's Bay which is dominated by the picturesque Elizabeth Castle.

Stafford Hotel

The Stafford Hotel is licensed for 149 guests and all the bedrooms are individually styled due to the recent extensive refurbishment. Each en-suite guest room has been well equipped, offering the guests colour TV, radio, direct dial telephones, tea and coffee making facilities and central heating. Your host Ian Bartlett and family have been welcoming guests to the Stafford Hotel for more than 70 years and it is this lifetime of personal experience that ensures you of individual service and attention. The atmosphere is one of warmth and friendship and Ian provides the kind of amenities that satisfy the many demands of the modern day tourist. The lounges are comfortably furnished and there are two inviting bars where you can sit and enjoy your favourite choice of beverage in the relaxed and pleasant atmosphere. Traditional English cuisine figures principally on the comprehensive menus and is created using only the finest local produce. Though you will find that there is sufficient variety in the dishes to remind the guest that they are, after all, outside the UK.

Jersey is renowned for its spectacular scenery, exhilarating walks and golden beaches, but for the more energetic there are golf courses to play and water sports galore to pursue. There are country lanes to explore, shops to visit and, in the evenings, a host of restaurants and bars in which to unwind, with mouth-watering food and tempting selections of fine wines. Jersey is well served by airlines, enjoying direct air-links with major airports in the UK and the Hotel offers attractive packages inclusive of air and ferry travel. Neighbouring fascinating destinations for day-trips with a Continental flavour, Jersey truly is a green emerald set in a diamond blue sea.

The Stafford Hotel, Kensington Place, St Helier
Tel: 01534 24953 Fax: 01534 23684

Situated on the corner of Halkett Street, near the Market Hall in the centre of bustling St Helier, **The Dog and Sausage** is an attractive local Inn which offers its visitors plenty of al fresco eating and drinking. The pub's official name was once the Dorset and Somerset which was derived from the railway of the same name. This then became locally known as the D & S which was eventually lengthened to the Dog and Sausage and the name has stuck over the years. At the turn of the century Jersey was home to many itinerant French farm labourers. They would descend on Hilgrove Street (also known as French Lane) every Saturday night, where

The Dog and Sausage

pubs and brothels were abundant, and spend all their weekly wages.

The exterior of the pub is covered with hanging baskets and window boxes of all descriptions and it is these displays that have won the Inn several local awards for excellence. Inside the pub lunches are quite superb, with most of the produce used being locally grown at nearby farms, so you can be assured of freshness. The varied and delicious menu consists of home-made pies, curries and lasagne, freshly made sandwiches are always available, with Jersey beef being the local speciality. Real ales, real atmosphere, real people and real food, if you enjoy the good life at a good price then look no further than The Dog and Sausage for a real Channel Island welcome.

The Dog and Sausage, Halkett Street, St Helier Tel: 01534 30982

If you are looking for a guest house that will offer you a taste of the good life in opulent and welcoming surroundings yet still provides you with all the comforts of home, then look no further than **La Bonne Vie**. This charming Victorian house was originally built for a local wealthy merchant and his family in the 1890s and is conveniently located only five minutes walk from St Helier and just a minutes stroll from the beach.

La Bonne Vie

Each guest room at La Bonne Vie has been individually decorated to a high standard with particular attention being given to the furnishings. Some of the bedrooms have beautiful antique brass beds, whilst others boast handmade French four-poster beds signed by their maker. All rooms have full en-suite facilities and include a television, tea and coffee maker, hairdryers, clock/radio and small necessity baskets as standard. The emphasis at La Bonne Vie is to provide the guest with a true home-from-home atmosphere, with an attention to detail that is truly second to none. Your hosts Carole and Ricci Hetherington lay out chocolates, biscuits and home-made fudge to greet you on your arrival and have created a quiet and relaxed ambiance that pervades throughout the house.

The pretty breakfast room offers you a hearty farmhouse breakfast, with home-baked muffins as a weekend speciality, and the cosy sitting room has an open feature fireplace for those wintry evenings. For five years running, La Bonne Vie has won the Gold Award for small gardens and this will come as no surprise to its many guests. Fresh flowers are in abundance throughout the house, visit in the long summer months and you will be rewarded by a riot of colour from the glorious hanging baskets that embellish the front of this fine guest house.

La Bonne Vie, Roseville Street, St Helier
Tel: 01534 35955 Fax: 01534 33357

Centrally situated in St Helier, just 150 yards from the sea front is the **Chelsea Hotel**, a large though friendly hotel well placed for the shopping centre, parks and various places of entertainment. The Chelsea is a ideal family Hotel with great facilities. For those who like fun in the sun, the large outdoor swimming pool and sun terrace will definitely be a big attraction, after which, a visit to the solarium might appeal. Entertainment is laid on four evenings a week during the main season and a children's game room helps to keep them occupied in idle moments. There are 114 bedrooms with private facilities all with colour television,

Chelsea Hotel

radio and baby listening service for guests with children.

The hotel has two bars, a comfortable cocktail/lounge bar and a ballroom bar. The service is friendly and helpful and, given the size of the Hotel, the staff are very attentive to the needs of guests. Good food has always been a tradition at the Chelsea Hotel with interesting and varied menus and a five course evening meal with a wide selection of wines to accompany your choice of meal. For those just wanting to relax, the Chelsea has a coffee shop and Bistro, a reading room and residents' lounge. A Travel Service is also operated by the Hotel who will book your hotel and travel in one easy transaction. They can arrange inclusive cost holidays to include air or sea travel and return transfers from Jersey Airport or Seaport to the Hotel, at very competitive prices.

Chelsea Hotel, Gloucester Street, St Helier
Tel: 01534 30241 Fax: 01534 66819

Cabbages and Kings opened at Red Houses in 1987 and moved into St Helier in 1992 just behind Queen Street in the Arcade. The name is derived from the poem by Lewis Carroll "The time has come, the Walrus said......". It is owner run by Mrs Sally Reading who packs this small shop with all sorts of interesting gift ideas, at a wide range of price levels, (of course there is no VAT). There is a wide selection of CATS - cushions, ceramics and wood with an ever changing range of glass, wood and ceramic items, plus select souvenirs.

The exclusive range of limited edition prints of Jersey and occasional original water colours is excellent and the pure silk flower buds in super colourways have been popular for many years. A particular delight is the collection of dolls' houses and miniature accessories which enchant even those who have not yet joined the rapidly growing band of devotees. Must not forget candles, burners, jewellery .... the list is so endless that you just have to experience for yourself the magic of Cabbages and Kings.

Cabbages and Kings, Queensway House, Arcade,
Queen Street, St Helier
Tel: 01534 33726

HISTORY OF JERSEY

The history of the Island is long and eventful and quite different from that of England. During the Stone Age, some 100,000 years ago, Jersey was a hunting ground for elephant and woolly rhinoceros and at La Cotte Cave, on the southwest coast at St Brelade, excavations found the remains of animal and human bones. It was not until 6500 BC that the melting of a giant ice cap separated the Channel Islands from the rest of Europe and to this day, at very low tide, the remains of a submerged forest can be seen in St Ouen's Bay.

Of the early discoveries the passage grave at La Hougue Bie is the most important and also, around this time, villages began to form as the hunter gave way to the farmer. Fragments of pottery and other household implements found around the Island resemble those found in northern France during the Iron and Bronze Ages. These were times of constant invasion as well and some defensive earthworks along the Island's coast date back more than 5000 years.

The Channel Islands fell to the might of the Roman invasion which swept across Europe in 56 BC though the Islands were left much to their own devices and there are few relics to be found from those times, just a few coins and trinkets.

During the relative peace of the early Christian era, the Islands were visited by St Sampson, St Brendan, St Helier and St Magliorus and the islanders were converted to Christianity. Parishes were set up and it is believed that many of the Island's churches were originally built at this time. However, the arrival of the Vikings in their long boats shattered this peace and a period of looting and murdering was begun. At this time too, Norse entered the language and the word ey, meaning island, provided the last syllable for Jersey, Guernsey and Alderney.

In AD 933 William Longsword, son of Rollo the leader of the most feared band of raiding norsemen, conquered Brittany and included the Channel Islands in his possession. It was Rollo who instituted the feudal system that remained in place for many centuries in one way or another.

William, Duke of Normandy and a descendant of William Longsword, conquered England at the Battle of Hastings in 1066 and so brought England under the same jurisdiction as the Channel Islands. It is still remembered on the Island that it was England that joined Normandy and became a possession of Les Isles Anglo-Normandes. It was the Normans that divided Jersey into fiefs, each with a Seigneur (Lord of the Manor) and it was also a policy of the Dukes of Normany to award their faithful followers with land. And so the de Carterets came from Normandy to their new estates in St Ouen.

When France finally conquered Normandy in 1204, the Islanders took the decision to remain loyal to King John who had offered them their own constitution as a reward. This was the foundation of the self-government and other priveleges that Jersey, and the other Islands, enjoy today. Though France, particularly in the 15th century, tried to regain its old possessions, the Channel Islands have remained British ever since and from the 16th century onwards they were only to be subjected to the invasion of pirates except for two notable periods, one in the 18th century and then again during World War II.

The last French attempt to capture Jersey was in 1781 when Baron de Rullecourt landed at La Rocque and marched to St Helier. The Baron was defeated in the Royal Square by a gallant Yorkshireman Major Francis Peirson who fell in the hour of victory and his opponent was mortally wounded. As a result of the Battle of Jersey, Fort Regent was built to protect St Helier but there was to be no further invasion by France.

At the outbreak of the Second World War, the Channel Islands were deemed by the British High Command to be of little interest to the invading German Army and so few measures were taken to protected the Islanders. By the time of Dunkirk, with the German Army only eight miles from Alderney, things looked less rosy and about half the population were evacuated, the remainder left defenceless. Finally invading in the summer of 1940, not a shot was fired in defence of this outpost of the British Empire. The German Occupation of the Islands lasted until the end of the War; a harrowing time for the population that ended on 8 May 1945. On all the Islands, except Alderney, 9 May is celebrated as Liberation Day. Reminders of the Occupation are visible all over Jersey and there are several museums which tell the story.

Rich in decor, ambiance and character, **The Revere** is a town hotel that is situated in the very heart of St Helier and only steps from the picturesque sandy beach. Originally a 17th century coach house, The Revere is steeped in history and character. The 50 individually styled bedrooms offer their guests the very best in luxury and comfort, with direct dial telephones and French and English Satellite TV. From the four-poster beds to the Spanish-style Bodega terrace and pool, it soon becomes clear that this is not just an Hotel, it is an experience that will enrich any stay on this beautiful Island.

The Revere

Locally renowned, the busy Candlelight restaurant offers an excellent quality of fresh produce and a fine wine cellar. Step into the Portcullis bar and enjoy an aperitif before entering the cosy wood panelled restaurant complete with antique table tops rosy with age. The flickering candles add to the warming effect, whilst the tempting menu guarantees that your meal will be an experience to be treasured.

Also situated in Kensington Place is **Doran's Courtyard Bistro**, an intriguing eating house hiding behind old warehouse windows and a huge wooden door. The relaxed world of Spanish style stone-flagged floors, old beams and pine antiques gives Doran's a cosmopolitan feel that attracts clientele as interesting and different as the restaurant itself.

Paul Doran and his chef Richard, seem to have trawled the world in his quest to bring together the different and divine; Prawn Risotto with a drizzle of Lobster Sauce and Fresh Parmesan shavings, Roast Breast of

Duck on a bed of Crispy Greens, Crystalised Ginger and Scallions with Plum Sauce rub shoulders with home-made pasta and pizza. For journeys into Jersey's beautiful countryside, the Revere Hotel is well situated with easy access to the Island's main artery roads and there is ample parking for 600 cars immediately adjacent.

The Revere, Kensington Place, St Helier
Tel: 01534 611111 Fax: 01534 611116

LE ROCQUIER

Samarès Manor is the third most senior manor in Jersey's hierarchy of manors and it dates back to Norman times. It takes its name from the saltpans (salse marais) that existed on the low-lying southern areas of the Island in medieval times. Though no-one knows who built the manor house seen today, some believe it to be Jacques Jean Hammond who purchased the property in 1754. However, there are small shreds of evidence that the house is older, particularly in the thickness of the building's walls. As early as 1680, the grounds of Samarès Manor were renowned for their trees and the magnificent gardens which delight today's visitors were laid out by Sir James Knott who bought the Manor in 1924. As well as touring the gardens, the internationally renowned herb garden and the manor house, younger visitors will enjoy the farm animals, including, of course, Jersey cows, and the horse-drawn carriage rides. The Manor also has a specialist plant centre, a craft centre and an excellent restaurant.

The passage grave, **Mont Ubé**, which stands on the hill of the same name, was discovered in 1848 and is dated from around 2500 BC. As with many dolmen, it had a capstone but that has long since been removed and during the 19th century the grave was used as a pigsty! Close by the dolmen is **Nicolle Tower**, a signal station built in 1792 that was used as a lookout during the German Occupation and is now owned by the Landmark Trust and makes interesting holiday accommodation.

PONTAC

Choosing the date at which to start a history can be more difficult in some cases than others, the history of **Pontac House** is one of those others. While the identity of its builder is not in doubt the exact date at which he ordered its construction remains elusive. In the circumstances we thought it best to start at the year in which his parents married and which, coincidentally marked the beginning of the 19th century. On 22nd November 1800 M David Gaudin married Mlle Marie Venement at St Clement's Parish Church. The groom hailed from the more northern parish of St Martin and the bride was the 36 year old eldest surviving daughter of M Daniel Venement and Mme Jeanne Touzel. Marie was presumptive heir to her only brother, the childless M Daniel Venement Jnr and, when he died in January 1808, Marie became owner of the estate. As David only had claim to a small farm in St Martin, this 29 year old ambitious farmer set about finding ways to consolidate his wife's legacy. Naturally the first lands that caught his attention were those immediately neighbouring his new home. Because of Marie's age, the Gaudins opportunities for having children were limited and out of the three children born to the couple, only one survived to adulthood. Born in 1804, their second son Daniel Gaudin grew to maturity and eventually married, the idea of buying a separate home for the family's sole heir must have occurred to David.

On 22nd May 1830, David went to the Royal Court to purchase a house with outbuildings, yards and land from his neighbour M Clement Touet. Although it is not possible to verify exactly when David and his young family took up residence in St Clement we are aware that they had settled there by the year 1815. This is known because records show that one David Gaudin of the Grande Vingtaine, St Clement appears in the Militia Census prepared for General Don. Daniel chose to follow in his fathers footsteps and marry a bride from St Clement, his first cousin Mlle Debora Venement. A coal merchant by trade, Daniel entertained ardent, civic ambitions and, in 1832, stood as the Rose, or Liberal Party Candidate, for office as Connetable of St Clement. Held on the 6th November, Daniel unfortunately lost out to Helier Godfray, who remained as Connetable until 1836.

Despite this initial frustration, Daniel finally reached the summit of his aspirations in 1839 when he became Connetable of St Clement, an office that he held until 1842. Once established as a prominent figure, Daniel felt the desire to build a new home which would both convey his status and create a favourable impression on visitors and fellow parishioners alike. This process began as early as 1833, with a raised loan from Mlle Esther Neel of 2295 livres. The property was built by 1839 and until 1917 was officially known as New Pontac, a house that is now known as La Fontaine and stands immediately to the west of Pontac House. Whether Daniel was merely unlucky, beleaguered by the schemes of opponents or simply spoilt, it is hard to tell but during the 1840s his financial hunger for credit led not only to his own downfall but deprived his mother of her title to her ancestor's farm. When Daniel began to flounder his mother sold rents secured on Beaumaris Farm to raise further funds and, in doing so, drew herself into the morass. Beaumaris Farm was sold in 1842 and, in 1845, New Pontac followed suit. Both properties were bought by M Jean Le Neveu, a cousin through marriage, and 86 year old widow Marie was allowed to stay in her home until her death, at 89, on 17th October 1853. Daniel had moved to No 12 St James's Street, St Helier shortly before selling New Pontac, though his troubles did not end there. In 1851 he met his financial nemesis when his entire estate was placed in the hands of his creditors and none other than Jean Le Neveu declared receiver. His fall came to its sorry conclusion on 1st March 1854 when he died of a stomach disease at 5 Peel Terrace in what is now the Route de Fort, St Helier. He was 49 years old.

The Pontac House Hotel

The conversion of New Pontac from an elegant residence to a hotel was surely the brainchild of Jean Le Neuve, the consummate businessman. On 19th April 1845, only seven days after Jean and Daniel stood before the Royal Court to exchange the freehold title of the property, the house opened its doors as a hotel under the management of Thomas Atkinson.

By 1851 Thomas Atkinson had been succeeded by another Englishman, John Tallis who was accompanied by his wife, Elizabeth Handley and their children Charles (then a clerk in the Royal Navy), Caroline, Eliza and Emma. The air of demure refinement established by Daniel Gaudin at great cost, was one that the new hoteliers went to great lengths to sustain. On 3rd April 1855 the Hotel was engraved by J Harwood of 26 Fenchurch Street, London, a fine portrayal of a house that clearly shows that a board declaring Tallis's New Pontac Hotel had been placed over the central window of the first floor. The loss of his wife in 1857 or his own failing health never precluded John's tireless efforts to nurture the Hotel's reputation and, in 1859, the last year of John's life, we find the New Pontac Family Hotel and Boarding House mentioned in *A Topographical & Historical Guide to the Island of Jersey.*

After his death on 11th June 1859, John was succeeded by his only son Charles, who managed the New Pontac Hotel at the time of the 1861 Census. After the death of M Jean Le Neveu in 1853 the freehold title passed to his only daughter and sole heir, Mlle Elizabeth Anne Le Neveu. Elizabeth, as the only child, enjoyed a substantial legacy and her husband, thus effective master of her estate, was her second cousin M Jean Le Neveu, third son of Jean Le Neveu gent. This second Jean belonged to the most senior branch of his family and he had inherited Seaforth Villa, a gracious property still standing today on the northern side of St Clement Coast Road. Articulate and intelligent, Jean became Connetable of St Clement in 1854 at the age of only 25, but despite his favourable beginning Jean was plagued with bad luck.

In 1863 Jean's wife died at the age of 27, leaving behind two small children for Jean to raise on his own. Ten years after that the principal business venture for which Jean is remembered went into liquidation. Around 1860 he formed a local bank by the name of Le Neveu Sorel & Co, an idea inspired by his prominent role in the St Clement Parish Bank from 1854-60. The bank subsequently acquired another local company, English and Jersey Union Bank. One of the banks directors was Henry Luce Manuel gent, notary and pioneer stockbroker, but in 1869 he chose to pull away from the bank and took a great many of the Bank's valued clients with him. This pushed Jean's company into terminal decline and on 24th September 1869, Jean Le Neveu sold the company and for the next 78 years New Pontac would revert to its original use as a private residence.

The new owner was Mlle Sara Hanna, little is known of this woman except that she was an absentee landowner. In the 1871 Census, New Pontac was inhabited by housekeeper Ann Halfield, who by 1881 had rented it out to a local rentier Adolphe Nicolle. But the practicalities of retaining the house must have been found wanting and on 10th December 1881 the house changed hands once more. It was purchased by M Josue Le Mottee, an unprepossessing rentier from St John. Born in 1829 Josue never left any definite impression on either the civic life or marital life of the Island and on 16th November 1896 he died of heart trouble. By 1902 his widow Mme Elizabeth Le Gallais, guardian of Josue's only son John Herbert Le Mottee sold it to its most nebulous owner.

The new resident was Jeanne Charlotte Augustine Jugla, born in 1860 she must have acquired her new home through the Island's myriad webs of friends that the Le Mottees adjoined. After 13 years Jeanne fell victim to cancer of the liver and on 2nd February 1915 she sold the property to Josue Renouf Bisson who, on the same day, sold the title back to Jeanne and her father, Alfred Hippolyte Romanin Jugla, on a joint basis to secure his position. On 5th June 1915 Jeanne finally died and a few weeks later her bereaved father sold the property to James Joslin Dupre.

James was a shopkeeper from St Helier and his tenure of the property was to be very short lived for within a year or two of buying the property, it soon became obvious that he had bitten off more than he could chew and defaulted on his loan. James was forced to sell the house to his bank manager to meet his debts and the man in question was James Bertram to whom the title passed on 21st April 1917. James was descended from the Bertram family of La Rocque, Grouville and educated in Victoria College. He rose from manager of the Savings Bank in New Street, St Helier (which now operates under the title of TSB Bank plc) to actuary. He died on 7th April 1942 when, under the terms of the deed of 1917, his widow Florence Eliza Maria Le Cornu became its sole owner. She, in turn followed her husband five years later and the property was inherited by her nephew Arthur Raymond Pepin.

Presumably Arthur could not put the house to any practical use and, on 20th December 1947, sold it to a man who would unwittingly turn it back to the use for which M Jean Le Neveu had bought it nearly 100 years earlier.

The new owner, Pierre François Rebindaine, has managed the Paddington Hotel in Cheapside and the Adelphi in St Helier, so the hotel business was no stranger. On the arrival of the German forces in 1940, Pierre evacuated to St Ives in Cornwall where he met his second wife Doris Emily Guest. On his return in 1945 he began to search for a place to re-establish himself in the hotel trade, Pontac House must have seemed perfect. As well as giving the property a face-lift, Pierre endowed it with a miniature Statue of Liberty which still stands on the front lawn today. At the beginning of 1967, Pierre and Doris retired and the property was sold to Robert Thomas Osborne Birkett and the house was transferred to corporate ownership not long afterwards. Now that the origins of the house are truly known, it is perhaps best that it should be remembered as a memorial to the dreams and hopes of its creator, Daniel Gaudin, for despite the highly publicised presence of the Tallis family neither they nor their successors could have succeeded without the ultimate product of Daniel's vision.

The Pontac House Hotel, St Clement's Bay Tel: 01534 857771

ST CLEMENT

This is the smallest of Jersey's parishes and its **Parish Church of St Clement** is probably dedicated to Clement I, the third pope. The oldest parts of the present church date from the 12th century and the church is unique on Jersey in have two carved piscinae both from the 14th century. Also in the churchyard is one of the Island's oldest memorial stones; bearing two dates, 1596 and 1606, and laid in memory of the Seigneurs of Samarès Manor. To the southwest of Church stood the Priory of St Clement, one of the six priories on the Island during medieval times and, typically, it was a small and humble institution.

The parish is famous as the one time home of Victor Hugo who fled to Jersey from France to escape persecution under Napoleon III. He lived with his family at Marine Terrace, which has since been demolished, until he was expelled from the Island for his inflammatory articles about Queen Victoria published in the *L'Homme* newspaper.

Situated just a few steps away from the attractive beach at **Grève D'Azette Bay** and only one mile from the islands main town, St Helier, **The Playa D'or** is most ideally situated for exploring this beautiful island. This three diamond guest house is under the personal supervision of the resident proprietors Angela and John Jeffery, a welcoming couple who make each and every guest feel at home. The Playa D'or offers its visitors a superb south facing sun terrace complete with tables, chairs and a spectacular view over the Bay of Grève D'Azette. This proves a very popular spot to sit and enjoy a drink whilst enjoying the heat on this sun soaked island.

There are fifteen well appointed bedrooms, each with full en-suite facilities, TV, hairdryers, radio/alarm and a complimentary tea and coffee tray. At the Playa D'or a good hearty breakfast is order of the day, choose between Continental fresh croissants and jam or a full English breakfast, all served by their friendly and attentive staff. The comfortable residents' lounge overlooks the sea and is where many guests choose to take afternoon tea, aperitifs or simply somewhere to unwind and relax after a busy day.

You will find numerous places of interest to visit nearby, try the world famous Jersey Zoo, the conservation dream of Gerald Durrell or Mount Orgueil Castle which boasts stunning views over the French coast. Whatever your pleasure, whether you enjoy dining in the best restaurants, partaking in a game of golf or tennis or simply exploring the miles of unspoilt countryside, The Playa D'or has all this and much more on its very doorstep.

The Playa D'or, Grève D'Azette, St Clement
Tel: 01534 22861 Fax: 01534 69668

GROUVILLE

Queen Victoria visited Jersey in 1859 and was so impressed with the sweep of this bay, which stretches from La Rocque Point to Gorey Harbour, that she decreed that it should be designated Royal. **Gorey Common**, which adjoins the beach, is home to the **Royal Jersey Golf Club**, founded in 1878 and one of the most picturesque links courses in Britain.

After the end of the American War of Independence eight Martello Towers were built on the shores of the Bay. The area around the square tower of **Fort Henry**, also known as La Tour Carree, on Gorey Common was a favourite place for duels in the 18th century. Whilst on one occasion soldiers garrisoned here were found to be making counterfeit coins.

Grouville Parish Church is dedicated to St Martin and the oldest parts remaining include the nave and its tower which date from the 12th or 13th century. There is unusual carved head, with a pierced forehead, set in a recess at floor level. Thought to be an aumbry, the curious position of the carving can be partly explained by the changes of floor level inside the church. Also of interest in the Church of St Martin de Grouville is the rare 15th century font. Carved from one single piece of granite it has a bowl within a bowl so that drops of holy water falling from the child's head may be caught.

Located on the Route des Sablons on the A4 next to the Royal Jersey Golf Course, the **Pembroke Hotel** is an attractive inn that is part of the Randalls Brewery chain. This family pub has been personally managed by Simon Critemery for the last four years and is featured in the nationally renowned Good Beer Guide. Food is served in the restaurant and bar area from 12 pm until 2 pm and 6 pm until 8 pm Mondays through to Saturdays with a set three course Sunday Lunch served from 1 pm until 2.30 pm.

The beer at Pembroke Hotel is excellent, with a wide range of Real Ales to choose from as well as the usual lagers, spirits and wines. There is a large and attractive beer garden to the rear of the Hotel and there is a good selection of facilities to keep the children entertained whilst you relax and enjoy a drink or a bite to eat. During the winter months, between October and March, a Quiz night is held in the bar every Thursday evening, giving locals and visitors alike the chance to pit their wits against each other to win the top prize. The Pembroke Hotel also has some excellent facilities for private parties and receptions with a large dining room and dance area for a good disco after your meal.

Pembroke Hotel, Route des Sablons, Grouville Tel: 01534 855756

GOREY

The harbour in this charming village was built in the early 19th century to cater for the needs of the oyster fishing industry that flourished here. In 1834 alone it was noted that 305,000 bushels of oysters were exported but, due to over-dredging, the industry began to decline after 1850. At the height of the oyster boom some 2000 men were employed in the task of collecting the oysters with many women and children ashore grading and packing the delicacies. Today the pretty little harbour is busy with privately owned yachts and boats. Overlooking the village and its harbour stands **Mont Orgueil**, a medieval castle built as a first line of defence against attacks from France. It is likely, however, that there has been a fortification, of sorts, on this site from as long ago as the Stone Age. The first documentary evidence of the present Castle dates from 1212, when King John granted to Philippe d'Aubigny 'the custody of Jersey and our Castle'. Over the years there were many additions to maintain the fortress as a first line of defence; the keep dates from the 13th century and Harliston Tower from the 15th century. However, by the time of the 1600s the Castle was becoming obsolete and Queen Elizabeth's engineer, Paul Ivy, recommended the building of a new fortress to replace Mont Orgueil and so Elizabeth Castle was built. Open daily from March to October, Mont Orgueil is one of the Island's most popular attractions and a series of tableaux tell the thousands of annual visitors the history within its walls.

Faldouet Dolmen

St Martin's Church

Jersey Pottery is unique to the Island and here visitors can watch every stage of the process from casting to decorating. With a popular restaurant and brasserie, which has been mentioned in 1996 Michelin Guide, there is something for everyone.

Lying to the northwest of Gorey is **Faldouet Dolmen**, a passage grave dating from around 2500 BC. Originally covered by an earth mound, which was removed in 1839, human remains were discovered here.

Jersey Diamond Centre

If you are visiting the magnificent Mont Orgueil Castle at Gorey on the east coast of Jersey, below the walls of the Castle you will find the **Jersey Diamond Centre**, home to the largest selection of diamond jewellery on the Island. The 1993 & 1995 Courtesy Award Winner, Jersey Diamond Centre is a real hidden gem. During your visit, you can see replicas of world famous diamonds worn by the rich and famous and, if your really lucky, take home the top prize in the Centre's Free Prize Draw, a £5000 diamond! Whether you are treating someone special or simply splashing out on yourself, Jersey Diamond Centre has the gem for the occasion. All prices are VAT free and there is a huge selection of jewels, each coming complete with a five year guarantee. The friendly, trained staff will offer you expert advice to help you make your choice and will even carry out alterations on your own jewellery. As well as the guarantee, you will also be given a certificate of purchase for insurance purposes and, if you wish, delivery to your hotel, now that's what I call service. So remember, if you are visiting this beautiful island add an extra sparkle to your holiday by discovering Jersey Diamond Centre at Gorey Harbour.

Jersey Diamond Centre, Gorey Pier Tel: 01534 851043
Fax: 01534 857192

ANNE PORT

Another of the Island's Martello Towers can be seen standing above Anne Port. Built in 1837, **Victoria Tower** was the last of this particular type of defensive structure to be constructed.

At the southern end of the bay is a large projecting rock known as Saut de Geoffroi or **Geoffrey's Leap**. In medieval times it was used as a place of execution where criminals were simply hurled down on to the rocks some way below. Legend has it that one particular criminal, having committed a crime against a woman, was sentenced to death from the rock. His name was Geoffrey and it is alleged that he survived the leap, a feat witnessed by the crowd that had gathered to see his death. He then decided to take the jump again, saying to a lady spectator "pour vos beaux yeux (on account of your beautiful eyes)". This time he was not so lucky.

ST CATHERINE'S BAY

The northern arm of the harbour, **St Catherine's Breakwater**, was constructed to protect the British Fleet and was begun in 1847. However, the water within the harbour proved to be too shallow for the ships and so the southern pier, on which stands Archirondel Tower, was never finished.

ST MARTIN

The earliest record of **St Martin's Church** dates from 1042 when William, then Duke of Normandy, granted it to Cérisy Abbey. Long regarded as the leading and richest church on Jersey, the Rector of St Martin's was often the Dean of Jersey, however, times have changed, and it is usual that the Dean of Jersey is also now the Rector of St Helier's. There is a memorial to the Reverend Charles Le Touzel, the rector here, who died in a bizarre riding accident. Whilst galloping home in the dark one stormy night, his horse collided with another going in the opposite direction. The Rector died of his injuries but there are no records telling of the other victims of the accident.

The Royal Hotel makes up the traditional trio of church, village shop and pub in the delightful village of St Martin. It is indeed a village pub, friendly, welcoming and very much a family pub where parents can take their children and where children are never bored because of the excellent outdoor play area with swings and slides and the indoor games room. But the Royal is also very much a local as is evident by the regulars who, lunchtime and evening, gather round the attractive lounge bar and exchange the day's news and gossip, forming what is affectionately known as The Office. At the same time the public bar is always fully patronised, mostly by the farm workers from the very agricultural parish which the Royal serves. There is no snobbishness or cliques at the Royal. Visitors are always made welcome and indeed many come back year after year because of the warm hospitality handed out by landlord John Barker and his excellent staff. Christian names are the order of the day and the sunny terrace in summer and roaring fire of the lounge in winter make both locals and visitors come back again and again.

The Royal Hotel

The food at the Royal Hotel is legendary in Jersey whether served downstairs in the bar and the non-smoking eating area, which opens out on to the extensive terrace, or in the separate restaurant upstairs where the same food is served at the same prices on pine tables in alcoves. The terrace extends the dining area in summer and is filled lunchtime and evening during the summer by diners in shorts and T-shirts. The Royal has a genuine country pub decor and atmosphere with horse brasses, bridle parts and old prints decorating the walls, yet the facilities are as up-to-date as anyone could wish for. The disabled are specifically catered for with ramps to all areas and a specially converted toilet. Well-kept and properly served real ale is on tap with Boddingtons being the permanent ale and the guest ales include Marston's Pedigree, Old Speckled Hen, Courage Directors and Old Peculiar. The lounge bar specifically excludes children so that adults without families can eat and drink in peace while families have the full run of the dining area, terrace and playground. With all this to offer, the Royal Hotel has one very special claim to fame, it is a pub with the feel, the hospitality and the food and drink of the real Jersey pub.

The Royal Hotel, Grande Route De Faldouet Fax: 01534 857298

ROZEL BAY

The name Rozel goes back to Norman times when a Seigneur from Rozel in Normandy had land on the Island. Coming from roseau, a reed, the form Roselle has become popular as a girl's name. The present **Rozel Manor** was built in 1770 by Charles Lemprière and, during additional construction work in 1820, Roman cement was uncovered on the site. The Manor's chapel is medieval though the internal furnishings of much later date.

Standing above the Bay can be seen **Le Castel de Rozel**, part of a great earthwork, originally a promontory fort, that dates from the Iron Age. Excavations have uncovered a number of Gaulish and early Roman coins dating from the 1st century BC and this suggests that the fort acted as a early defensive position against attack and, possibly, as a home to refugees from Gaul. It was from Rozel Bay, in 1830, that Jersey's first lifeboat was launched.

When travelling through St Martin, be sure to make a bee line for **The Rozel Bay Inn** which is run by licensee, Mrs Eve Bouchet. The gourmet fayre that is served at this superb pub, has earned it national recognition and the 1996 Good Pub Guide's, Best Dining Pub of the Year. The Inn has an exciting and inspiring menu with a wide selection of more unusual dishes created by the in house chefs David Romanis and Derek Woods. The choice of main courses usually includes lots of local fresh fish as well as meat and vegetarian options are available on request. On the evening à la carte menu, the starters could include Veal and Smoked Bacon Terrine with a Tarragon Dressing and Chargrilled Vegetables with Parmesan and Salsa Verde. For your main course there are such dishes as Noisettes of Lamb with a Rich Caramelised Shallot and Basil Sauce or Steamed Fillet of Sea Bass with a Chervil, Dry Vermouth and Lime

Sauce. And if you still have room for a dessert, there is Iced Drambuie Parfait with a Praline Anglais, what more can I say except bon appetit! For those only needing a quick snack, Pub Grub is also available from the bar and on fine days can be eaten at the tables outside this decidedly accomplished Inn.

Rozel Bay Inn, La Vallee de Rozel, St Martin Tel: 01534 863438

TRINITY

The largest parish on the Island, **Holy Trinity Parish Church**, to give it its correct name, dates from the 12th century, though the nave was rebuilt in 1865. The Church contains the only piece of pre-Reformation silver to have survived on Jersey; a chalice with an eight-lobed base. Housed in a converted Methodist Chapel dating from 1833 is the **Sir Francis Cook Gallery**. Sir Francis used the chapel as a studio and, following his death in 1978, it was donated to the Jersey Heritage Trust for use as a gallery by his widow. It contains a permanent exhibition of the artist's work as well as a wide range of temporary exhibitions.

Perhaps the most famous attraction on Jersey is **Jersey Zoo**. Founded 30 years ago by Gerald Durrell it is the headquarters of the Jersey Wildlife Preservation Trust and is a unique sanctuary and breeding centre. The 25 acres of parkland and water gardens provide natural surroundings and habitats for some of the world's rarest species, in fact, some are so rare that they may only be seen in Jersey. A major part of the Zoo's work is the reintroduction of animals to the wild and for some Jersey is only a temporary home before they are released back into the wild. The work of the Trust extends to all the four corners of the world and they have had universal acclaim in Mauritius, Majorca and Brazil as well as aided conservation programmes in India, Madagascar and the Caribbean. The Zoo has a programme of special activities specially designed for children which run from April to August.

Near the Parish Church is another splendid establishment, the **States Experimental Farm**. As well as offering a modern scientific advice service, the Farm conducts experimental work into all aspects of agriculture. The Farm was originally the gift of TB Davis and was given in memory of his son who died in the First World War.

Orchids are a worldwide passion and this 'Royal Family of Plants', with more than 20,000 species, makes up one of the largest families of flowering plants in the world. Down the ages mankind's fascination for orchids has rivalled that of precious metals and stones and orchids have often been valued above rubies and other beautiful but sterile objects. Orchids are living beings and there is intense competition amongst breeders which is channelled into the production and development of new hybrids, resulting in stunning shapes, colours and flower sizes.

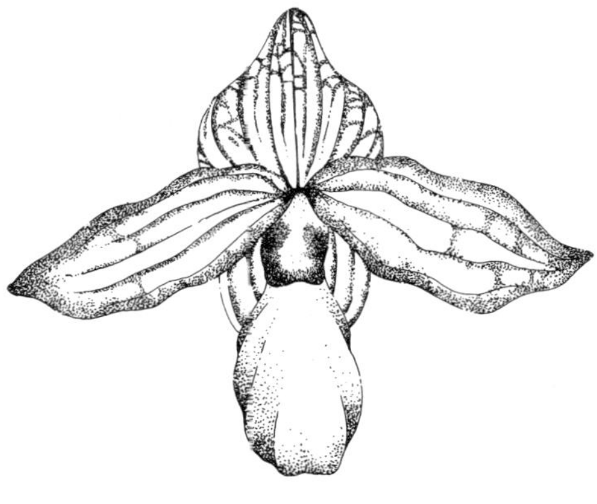

Paphiopedilum 'Gloria Naugle' Slipper Orchid

What is internationally acknowledged to be one of the finest collections of orchids in the world is to be found at **Eric Young Orchid Foundation** at Victoria Village, Trinity. The collection was established in 1958 by Eric Young, a trained scientist and keen horticulturist from childhood. Within ten years it was believed to be the finest private collection of orchids in Europe, if not the world. But this was not to be a private passion. Eric Young's dream was to set up a foundation to maintain his collection in perpetuity to enable visitors to benefit from its splendour and excellence. The collection is maintained and developed inside a series of heated glasshouses, comprising five growing houses and a display house. The display house is open to the public and features permanently planted landscapes creating an exotic environment using raised beds, traditional Jersey granite, logs and branches, designed to show the orchids in their extravagant beauty.

The Eric Young Orchid Foundation, which regularly participates in international festivals bringing home major awards, is open throughout the year on Thursdays, Fridays and Saturdays, from 10 am to 4 pm.

Eric Young Orchid Foundation, La Rue Du Moulin, Du Ponterrin, Trinity Tel: 01534 861963

If you are one of the many people in this country who is fascinated in steam engines and enjoys the smell of the grease and oil, then **The Pallot Heritage Steam Museum** is definitely the place for you. The Museum lies between the A8 and A9 main roads (bus route 5 is easiest) and is signposted off both roads. Come and see the wide variety of preserved steam engines, vintage farm equipment, church and cinema organs and much, much more. Lyndon 'Don' Pallot was the founder of this stunning museum and he spent much of his early days as a trainee engineer with the old Jersey Railway. It was much later on, when he was working as an agricultural and contracting engineer, he began to collect what he

The Pallot Heritage Steam Museum

could of our mechanical and farming heritage. There is no doubt that but for Don's steady interest that was maintained over many years, much that is on view today would have been lost forever.

The recently completed Victorian train station is a replica of what would have been used over 100 years ago and on Thursdays, (Tuesdays and Thursdays from mid June to mid September) the clock is turned back and you may travel by steam hauled carriages from the platform of the Victorian style station. On show amongst the many displays that you will find is a 1912 church pipe organ and a 1938 eight rank Compton theatre organ which was once used daily in the Odeon, Guernsey. You will find The Pallot Heritage Steam Museum is an absorbing evocation of times past with something to excite the interest of everyone in this fascinating collection of steam, farm and other machinery.

The Pallot Heritage Steam Museum, Rue de Bechet, Trinity
Tel: 01534 865307 Fax: 01534 865506

Located one mile north of St Helier on the Trinity Hill (A8) in quiet and rural surroundings, **The Blacksmiths Arms** is a popular pub that stands adjacent to The Oaklands Lodge Hotel. The Lodge is a small, modern hotel whose aim is to provide its guests with every comfort and service. The attractive Tavern Bar is oak panelled with classic leather upholstered chairs, the perfect place for relaxing and enjoying a drink from the exotic Cocktail bar or selecting your meal from the extensive and varied menu.

The Blacksmiths Arms

The Blacksmiths Arms is owned by the well known Randalls Brewery chain and has been managed for the past five years by your most excellent host, Joe Graca. The two bars are frequented by both locals and visitors alike who come to enjoy the jovial ambiance that is created by the unique character and atmosphere that each bar possesses. There are eight twin and two double guest bedrooms, each being luxuriously appointed with private bathroom, telephone, colour TV, clock radio and complimentary tea and coffee making facilities.

Making up the trio of Hotel, Inn and Eating House is the Red Rose Restaurant, winner of many awards during the annual Jersey Good Food Festival. Relax in elegant surroundings and select your meal for the evening from the excellent table d'hôte menu which is available to those residents on half board, or the superb Gastronomic Restaurant menu and extensive wine list. Traditional Sunday Lunch is served every weekend and you can also enjoy a meal at lunchtime throughout the week with the special Table d'hôte lunch menu. What more could you ask for but to be surrounded by picturesque countryside, yet still be only a stones throw from one of the best pubs and restaurants on the Island, perfect.

The Blacksmiths Arms, Augres, Trinity
Tel: 01534 861735 Fax: 01534 864839

LA HOUGUE BIE

Described as "one of Europe's finest prehistoric monuments", this great burial ground covers a Neolithic tomb which dates from 3000 BC. Visitors can walk around the passage grave and also up to the two medieval chapels on the site. The western chapel was built by early missionaries and is dedicated to **Notre Dame de la Clarté** (Our Lady of Light) whilst the eastern chapel is known as the **Jerusalem Chapel**. Beneath it is a crypt which contains a representation of the Holy Sepulchre in Jerusalem. Throughout the middle ages this was a place of pilgrimage and the name actually comes from the old Norse for mound (haugr) and settlement (bu).

The 20th century is also represented here in the concrete bunker built by the Germans as a communications centre and in which is now housed a collection of military artefacts. The interactive Discovery Centre helps visitors young and old get a real feel for the history of this ancient site and it is open daily from March to October.

ST SAVIOUR

The **Parish Church**, which dates from the 12th century, is often known as St Saviour of the Thorn, but his name did not appear until 1646. Like many of the parish churches on Jersey, little remains of the original medieval construction and, again a typical feature of the Island's churches, it was heavily restored in Victorian times (in this case in 1895). Of the memorials in the churchyard, the one that is of most interest to visitors is that of Lillie Langtry. The daughter of Dean Le Breton, 'Jersey Lily' was the most celebrated beauty of her time and the toast of London Society. **Government House**, built in 1817, has been the home of the Lieutenant-Governor since 1822.

To the west of the town lies **Queen's Valley**. One of the most beautiful and least spoilt valleys on the Island, it has the alternative name of La Vallée des Moulins (the Valley of the Mills) and indeed, three watermills where were recorded as early as 1274, can be found along its length. Both Victor Hugo, in 1855, and George Eliot some two years later, have written of the peace and tranquillity of this glorious valley.

Champ Colin

Set amidst the green and fragrant countryside, ten minutes drive from St Saviour town centre, **Champ Colin** guest house offers its guests an escape from the hustle and bustle of everyday life. Relax in the tranquil atmosphere that pervades throughout this 17th century house. Originally a farmhouse, Champ Colin became a guest house in 1981 and has been owned and personally run by Mr and Mrs Buesnel ever since. This superior house still boasts many of its original features including a granite Jersey fireplace in the attractive dining room and traditional circa 1800s furniture in every room.

There are three en-suite guest bedrooms, each having been individually decorated and furnished to a very high standard. Also provided for your pleasure is a colour TV, full central heating and tea and coffee making facilities with a large half tester bed to aid your relaxation. Each morning a generous English breakfast is served in the light and airy dining room and can be followed by a walk around the large and picturesque gardens that surround this beautiful guest house. Owing to its central location it is easy to visit a whole host of local amenities including the nearby sandy beaches and the colourful boutiques and restaurants of St Saviour and St Helier. Because of the care and attention that is lavished upon each and every visitor to Champ Colin we can guarantee that you will wish to return again and again to this haven of peace and tranquillity.

Champ Colin, Rue du Champ Colin, St Saviour Tel: 01534 851877

The East

ST AUBIN

Though the town was once the commercial centre of Jersey, it has never been its capital. The prosperity of St Aubin is based around its harbour and its trade with, in particular, Canada. Fishing fleets bound for the Newfoundland Cod Banks would shelter in the harbour at the jetty constructed in 1670. Money raised from wines and spirits paid for the construction of the south harbour arm in 1699 but it was not until 1819 that the northern arm was built by Jean Janvrin. However, the building of the new harbour at St Helier in the 1840s saw a decline in the importance of St Aubin.

The days of prosperity can still be seen by today' visitors in the unusual Merchants' Houses which rise to four or five storeys instead of the more common and modest two storeys. The elegance of the place remains too and it is a much favoured holiday centre, away from the bustle of St Helier.

The 17th and 18th centuries were, though, not all peaceful as this was the age of piracy. Captured enemy ships were brought to the harbour and sold, an activity which centred around the Old Court House. Whilst shipbuilding has been carried out at St Aubin since the 17th century, it was not until the 19th century that it became significant.

The town is named after St Aubin, Bishop of Angers, who died in around 550. A protector against pirates, there is no evidence of a church or a chapel dedicated to him though it is thought that there was once a chapel on the islet on which now stands **St Aubin's Fort**. There has been a fortification here since about 1542 and its position, just outside the harbour, made it an ideal complement to Elizabeth Castle in defending St Helier and St Aubin. Over the years there have been many additions and modifications though, in fact, the Fort has never been used in war. The Germans used St Aubin's Fort and heavily fortified it and it can be reached, at low tide, on foot. During the Occupation, the Germans also heavily fortified **Noirmont Point**, on the extreme west of the Bay. Their bunkers, along with the panoramic views, can still be seen.

Tucked away in the back streets of St Aubin behind the picturesque harbour on Le Quai Bisson directly behind Le Bon Viveur Restaurant you will find **Abracadabra**. This unique Craft and Maritime Centre is an Aladdin's cave of gifts and treasures from all around the world. Delightfully different, Abracadabra is a kaleidoscope of colour from the moment that you step through the door with every gift being bright, exciting and imaginative. Ranging from novelties, toys and ornaments to colourful mobiles and windchimes, you are guaranteed to find just the right gift for that special someone.

Abracadabra
Unique Crafted
Gifts

You will also find a selection of crafts by local artists and the more traditional souvenirs including the famous Jersey Mooing Cows! For a trip down memory lane look no further than the Gallery, featuring a range of fascinating pictures of the old railway and enchanting views of St Aubin from days gone by. So when visiting this beautiful part of Jersey, Abracadabra is the one place that you are guaranteed to find the perfect present to remember your stay in the Channel Islands.

Abracadabra, Craft & Maritime Centre, Le Quai Bisson, St Aubin
Tel: 01534 490392

A true family run establishment situated at St Aubin's Harbour, a truly historic part of Jersey, **Pebbles Guest House** is pleasantly small and has been run by Steven Houiellebecq and his wife Cass since 1982. As they have two children themselves, Steven and Cass welcome families with children of all ages. And continuing the family feeling, Steven's mother resides next door at La Poste which offers visitors to this beautiful island self-catering accommodation. On arrival at Pebbles Guest House, you will immediately be greeted by a friendly welcome and be taken to one of the five rooms available, each having been tastefully decorated with a TV and complimentary tea tray.

Pebbles Guest House

The full English breakfast is served in the attractive dining room and includes a selection of home-made jams and marmalades spread thickly on Steven's home-baked bread. On display throughout the house is an abundance of art work including paintings and bronzes, each having been created by Steven and can be purchased as a keepsake of your stay in Jersey. If painting or sculpture is of interest to you, then tuition is available if requested on application. For your enjoyment there is a TV and games lounge complete with snooker table to keep the children fully occupied and there is also free admission to a variety of evening entertainment at nearby hotels.

Pebbles Guest House, Market Hill, St Aubin
Tel & Fax: 01534 43547

PORTELET BAY

The little island in the Bay is crowned by the round tower of **Janvrin's Tomb**. It was here that the Captain was laid to rest following his death from the plague. He was later buried in St Brelade's Church.

Old Portelet Inn

Originally built in 1606, **Old Portelet Inn** is a family pub that has been managed by Tina Lister for the past six years and is a credit to her warm and friendly personality. This family pub is filled with plenty of olde world charm and comes complete with traditional wooden beams and local memorabilia. From the balcony in the upstairs area of the bar, you will be treated to a fabulous view out over the picturesque Portelet Bay, the perfect place to sit and enjoy a cold glass of wine and a good chat. This huge pub has no less than three bars, one of which is a family room where the children can roam free. Also for the children is a Pirate Pete's inside and an outside play area, allowing the kids to entertain themselves while you relax with a drink and something delicious to eat. Food is served between 12 pm and 9 pm seven days a week and can be eaten inside in the bar areas, restaurant or you could take it al fresco and enjoy your meal in the large beer garden at the front of the Inn. During the long summer months the Old Portelet Inn has plenty of live music every night of the week, whilst in the winter you will be able to catch a live local band once a week on selected evenings. This superb pub is owned by the renowned Randall Brewery and offers something for any traveller who happens to frequent this friendly and welcoming tavern.

Old Portelet Inn, Portelet Bay Tel: 01534 41899

ST BRELADE

The Bay here has been described by the famous globe-trotter and Jersey resident, Alan Whicker, as one of the loveliest in the world. The **Parish Church**, dedicated to St Brelade, a companion of St Sampson, was mentioned in a deed signed by William, Duke of Normandy prior to 1066; so the date of the church's construction, given in so many guidebooks as 1111, is inaccurate. The oldest part of the church, the chancel, dates from the 11th or early 12th century, with the tower and nave being some 100 years younger. Situated close to the church is **The Fisherman's Chapel** which dates from the late 12th century. There was probably a chapel here as early as the 6th century and this would make the chapel the oldest site of worship on the Island. Like the church of St Brelade, the stained glass is also by HT Bosdet, a local craftsman and the windows depict the life of St Brendan.

Jersey Lavender is a working farm with carefully tended plants that is a riot of colour from the beginning of the summer; harvesting takes place from June to August and the smell is heavenly. The Farm has remained a friendly and personal local enterprise, the lavender is distilled and bottled here and all manner of toiletries are also produced. Visitors can tour the farm and bottling plant, rub, dab and sniff the samples and watch a video describing the whole process from young plant to bottle perfume. The Farm is open Monday to Saturday, from the end of May to the end of September. Another true labour of love, the **Shell Garden** was created by a gifted amateur couple and is now one of the sights of Jersey. Monies raised from visitors go to charity.

Perched high above the Ouaisné headland in Jersey, just before the road to Portelet Common becomes a pot-held track, lies **Morgan Pottery**.

Everything has been made and decorated by Kim Morgan, a New Zealander who married a local Jersey girl, Debbie, after a weekend trip to visit his girlfriend simply stretched and the couple married and settled on the Island.

The workshop was established in 1993 and sells a large range of domestic ware and one off individual pieces. Kim prizes function nearly as highly as beauty in his work, and all cookware is safe to use in the oven, microwave and dishwasher. Tiki the Red Setter is the first to greet a visitor on their arrival to Kim's garage workshop, and many people come to watch the artist at work and purchase some of his beautiful hand thrown stoneware. Many of the designs that embellish the pottery are fine examples of Kim's pure approach to his work, rhythmic shapes and restrained patterns work in harmony with the delicately soothing glazes. In the vases and plates you will notice an element of Japanese style, with its fluid simplicity and fragile colour, each piece is created from experience and often a little Zen. The showroom is open all year round from 10.00 am until 6.00 pm and offers its visitors probably the best display of unique, hand-made pottery on the Island.

LE CORBIERE

The name comes from the French word carbeau meaning a haunt of crows or ravens, both birds of bad omen. Indeed, the reef here is treacherous and has long been the scene of shipwrecks. The first mention of such a disaster was 1309 and legend has it that in 1414 a Spanish ship floundered here and the whole area was covered with casks of wine. The rocks are mainly pyramidal in shape and some tower to over 100 feet above sea level. Accessible at low tide great care should be taken as the tide sweeps in with great speed. Considering the danger posed by the rocks it is surprising that it was not until 1873 that **Le Corbière Lighthouse** was built, towering over the jagged rocks. Le Corbière is a popular place from which to watch the sun set over the Atlantic Ocean.

Enjoying a unique and spectacular location on the extreme south west cliffs of Jersey, **Le Chalet Hotel** and Restaurant boasts views over

Corbière Lighthouse, an important local landmark, and the picturesque St Ouen's Bay. Le Chalet has been a hotel since the turn of the century and in the 1920s proved a very popular destination to spend the afternoon sipping champagne and enjoying a lobster tea.

All of the Hotel bedrooms have seaviews and are individually furnished and styled to a high standard, offering the visitor satellite television, direct dial telephone, full en-suite facilities and room service complete with baby-sitting option if needed. The restaurant, bars and function rooms are popular with both the locals and tourist alike, with many non-residents regularly making reservations to dine and enjoy the spectacular sunsets. Le Chalet Restaurant specialises in an abundance of local seafood and provides a comprehensive and varied menu prepared by the in-house award winning chef. There is an excellent selection of fine European wines available, and cocktails can be served on the restaurant terrace while you sit and listen to the rhythmic lapping of the waves on the rocks below. Whether it is your Wedding Reception, a gala dinner, or an anniversary party, Le Chalet will provide the ultimate setting, a professional service and a variety of menus to suit the occasion. All guests are welcome to either relax by the Hotel swimming pool, enjoy a game of tennis on the Hotel tennis court, play a round of golf or simply take a walk along the many coastal paths around Corbière.

Le Chalet Hotel and Restaurant, Corbière, St Brelade
Tel: 01534 41216 Fax: 01534 47144

ST PETER

First mentioned in 1053, the **Parish Church of St Peter** had a priory situated close to it that survived until 1461, and was not confiscated by the Crown in 1413 as were many of the Island's priories. The western

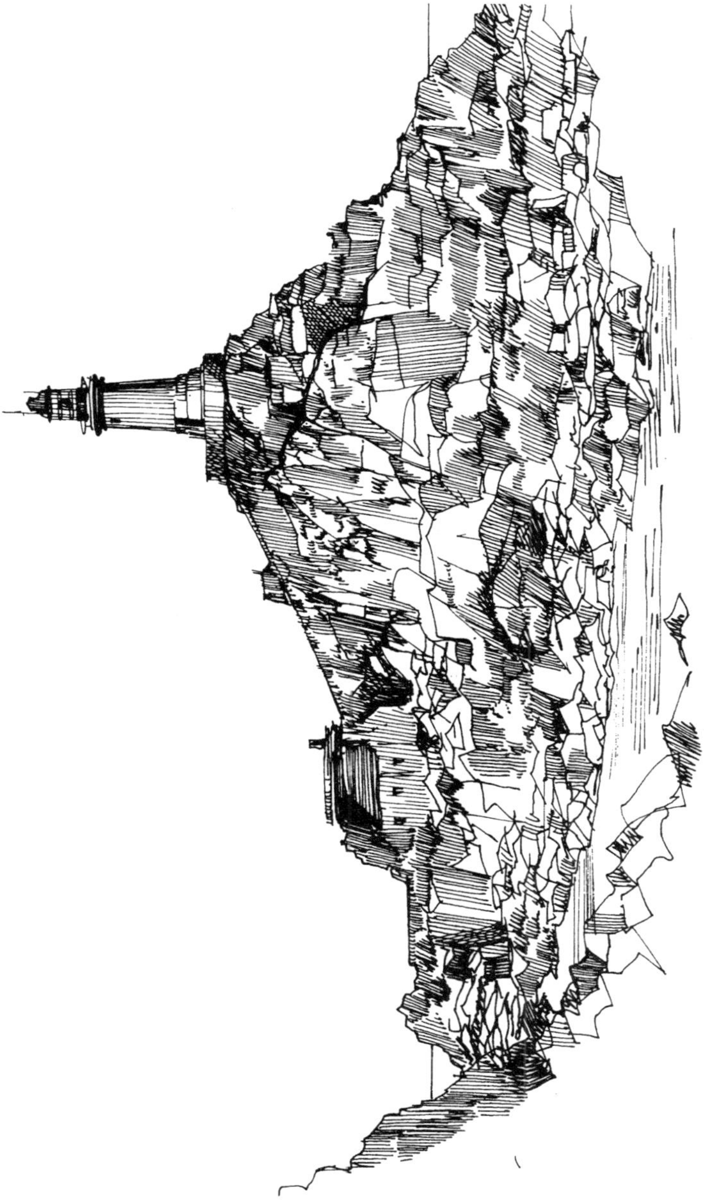

Corbière Lighthouse

area of the parish is largely sand dunes and this has given rise to its name, St Pierre dans le Désert. The inland areas are of valleys and pasture.

Out in St Ouen's bay stands **La Rocco Tower**, the last of Jersey's round towers to be built in 1800. It was severely damaged during the Second World War and the further actions of the sea and weather reduced it to a ruin. It was restored in 1970.

The Jersey Motor Museum, open daily, has a whole range of military vehicles, veteran and vintage cars and motorcycles on display and includes the Rolls-Royce Phantom III that was used by General Montgomery whilst he was planning the D-day landings. Close by is the **St Peter's Bunker Museum** which has the largest collection of German militarian and civilian occupation relics on the Island. The Museum is open daily from April to October.

One of the loveliest spots on the Island must be **St Peter's Valley**. At one time the stream running through it supported six water mills and, during the German Occupation, some were pressed back into service. **Le Moulin de Quétivel**, first recorded in 1309, has been fully restored by the National Trust and it makes an interesting visit. To the north of the watermill is **The Living Legend**, a recreation of a village which reflects the Island's history and also its unique government. With plenty to see and do for all the family it makes a great day out.

Situated in the heart of Jersey's largest conservation area, St Ouen's Bay, **Les Mielles Golf and Country Club** welcomes golfers of all standards at this newly developed course. Ten years ago heavy demand for tee-times at Jersey's other three golf clubs gave Jonathan le Brun the idea of extending a former nine hole par three course, opened on the Les Mielles marshlands by his grandfather, Jack A'Court, into a full 18 hole course. The American style layout is designed with a number of water hazards, high quality 'bent grass' greens and fairways of dwarf ryes and was once described by professional Jeremy Phillips as, "as unforgiving a course as you could play - it teaches you how to play your way around a golf course, not hit your way around". The course is open to all golfers who are in possession of a handicap certificate, or green card equivalent and a high standard of dress is required.

There is a 30 bay driving range available, 20 covered and 10 open, for practice or tuition by Jeremy Phillips, NZPGA, and an essential putting green and practice bunker. The standard of amenities is first class with showers and changing facilities, bar and restaurant where children are always welcome, al fresco patio with seasonal barbecue, and the Channel Island's largest Pro Shop. The shop is VAT free and stocks a large and varied range of equipment and accessories including, Lynx, Ping, Titleist, Wilson and Callaway and MacGregor. Since it was first opened Les Mielles has spearheaded package golf holidays on Jersey, and the Le Bruns deal with a number of different tour operators and package holiday companies. There is a pre-booked tee-off time in operation at Les Mielles, so it is necessary to call for your reservation to avoid disappointment and Golf clubs, carts and buggies can be hired on the premises.

Les Mielles Golf and Country Club, St Ouen's Bay, St Peter
Tel: 01534 482787

ST OUEN

This is the largest parish on the Island and it covers the northwest corner of Jersey. The **Church**, dedicated to St Ouen (pronounced one) or Owen, Bishop of Rouen in 639, has as its oldest parts the nave, tower and chancel which date from the 12th and 13th centuries. The unusual staircase, which must have replaced the original medieval one, leads up to the tower and, unique to Jersey, are the round arches in the south aisle.

To the east of the Parish Church lies **St Ouen's Manor**. There has probably been a manor house here before 1135 when the de Carteret family, from Normandy, are thought to have come to the Island. However, it was not until 1204 that the family, relinquishing their lands on the Continent, lived on the Island permanently. The magnificent stately home has been in the family ever since and, though its opening times are restricted it is well worth a visit. The oldest part is the south tower which was built in 1380 and the west and north wings were added in the 16th century. Built in the early 14th century, **St Anne's Chapel**, in the Manor grounds, has been used as a barn and during the Occupation acted as a storehouse and a butchery.

Sir George Carteret, of the original de Carteret family, was one of Charles II's staunchest supporters and, following the Civil War in 1664, he was granted lands in America from a grateful sovereign. These lands Sir George named New Jersey and he was also a founder of the famous Hudson Bay Company.

The **Battle of the Flowers Museum** is owned and run by Miss Bechelet, who has exhibited at every Battle of the Flowers since 1934. There is a taped commentary telling the history and tradition of the festival as well as displays which bring the colourful event to life. Visitors can also see the grasses and wild flowers that Miss Bechelet grows for use in her floats.

The **Jersey Shire Horse Farm and Museum** is one of the most popular tourist attractions in the Channel Islands and is located at Champdonne near St Ouen. If you are travelling from the St Helier area, then the number 8 bus route stops directly outside the farm gates, so what could be simpler. The Jersey Shire Horse Farm is open from March through to October and offers its visitors a true farmyard experience. There is something for everyone, for the younger members of the family you will find a whole host of Shetland ponies, donkeys, a herd of goats, sheep, pigs and rabbits. You can see the magnificent Shire horses and the young foals which are born each year at the centre. There is a superb collection of horse-drawn vehicles, farm implements and harnesses, and you can experience the past by taking a carriage ride in the farm's traditional Jersey horse-van.

Jersey Shire Horse Farm and Museum

Every Wednesday you will be able to watch the resident farrier shoe the horses, then take time out to explore the Agricultural Museum which is packed with interesting bygone memorabilia. The old farmhouse serves delicious cream teas, ploughman's lunches and a large range of snacks, whilst adjoining the tea-room there is a delightful tea-garden with a play area for the kids. The Jersey Shire Horse Farm and Museum can keep a whole family entertained for hours, and having been awarded the Jersey Tourism Courtesy Award, you can be sure of a warm and friendly welcome.

Jersey Shire Horse Farm and Museum, Champdonne, Route de Trodez, St Ouen Tel: 01534 482372

The **Sunset Carnation Nurseries** are situated within walking distance of the Atlantic breakers on the Island's west coast, along the unmade road leading off Five Mile Road that skirts past Les Mielles Golf Course. The long hours of sunshine and mild climate make Jersey the ideal location for this superb two acre flower farm. Stuart Simon, the owner of Sunset Carnation, has family links with this nursery right back to circa 1930 when his grandfather started farming potatoes and tomatoes before the war. This was taken one step further by Simon's father who began growing daffodils in the 1940s and the carnation nursery that you see before you today began planting in 1973 and was opened to the public in 1975.

Sunset Carnation Nurseries

This marvellously coloured and perfumed flowering paradise has 100,000 square feet of under glass planting, filled with a profusion of carnations and the orchid-like alstroemeria, also called the Peruvian Lily. Every morning the flowers are picked just as the buds begin to open, they are then stood in a special solution which increases the vase life by up to ten days. Many varieties of carnation are grown including some very unusual colours.

Also in this spectacular floral setting is an indoor Tropical Bird Garden with a fine selection of feathered friends including the tiny Zebra finches to the colourful Macaw's and Cockatoos, all flying free amongst the exotic plants, flowers and fish pools. In the flower and gift shop you will find plenty of seeds and bulbs including the Jersey Lily and a select range of gifts and souvenirs. The Sunset Tea Garden offers a selection of delicious home-made savoury snacks, light lunches, cakes and teas. Open from April 1st until the end of October, admission is free with a modest charge to enter the Tropical Bird Garden and you will find plenty of free parking space on the premises. Whilst visiting the Sunset Carnation Nurseries you can place a flower order to be delivered to any address in Great Britain and Western Europe and even request deliveries for future birthdays or special events.

The Sunset Carnation Nurseries, St Ouen Tel: 01534 482090

L'ETACQ

Situated to the northwest of St Ouen's village and at the northern end of St Ouen's Bay, the village's name is derived from the Norse 'Stakkr' which means a heap or stack. There is a forest embedded in the Bay at this point which was last uncovered during an exceptionally low tide in 1903.

The **Channel Island's Military Museum**, overlooking the Bay, is housed in a German bunker and has collections of both German and British military relics from the time of the Occupation. Close by, however is a very different collection which is equally fascinating. **Microworld** is dedicated to the world of miniature objects and amongst its minute displays is the world's smallest violin, built by Cornel Schneider and just 37 mm long.

Surrounded by idyllic countryside on the Five Mile Road in St Ouen's Bay, **Jersey Goldsmiths** offers something of interest for all the family. Set in the middle of bright and colourful flowerbeds and lawns, Jersey Goldsmiths offers you the chance to view one million pounds worth of gold and also measure your weight in gold. The children will love to explore the exciting Pirates Trail, a great competition that leads to a free gift if completed. Happy staff mean happy customers and Irene, the manager, confirms that a Jersey Goldsmiths clients come first. The pleasant and helpful staff, who between them have years of experience and an in-depth knowledge of their products and precious metals in general, are at your disposal to give advice and guide you through the fabulous jewellery and items on show. This family owned business has a customer care service that is second to none and will even let you view certain items outside in the gardens so that you can truly appreciate the luster of gold in the daylight.

Gold has been used in the creation of beautiful and valuable jewellery for over 6000 years and as it never tarnishes or corrodes, its beauty never diminishes while its value continues to appreciate. During your visit to this 24 carat attraction you will discover the largest display of gold jewellery in the Channel Islands. This unique collection offers a combination of design and value to suit all tastes and purses, and with modern fashion in mind, the jewellery is crafted in both gold and hard rolled gold. One area of particular interest to the visitor is the workshop, here you can watch the goldsmiths creating some of the wonderfully intricate jewellery that you have seen in the showroom. The craftsmen will also accept commission work and will design to your individual requirements whilst they are always happy to alter and repair a visitor's own jewellery if they so wish.

Jersey Goldsmiths, Five Mile Road, St Ouen
Tel: 01534 482098 Fax: 01534 864839

The garden terrace which surrounds the beautiful fountain and goldfish pond is the perfect place to relax and enjoy a cup of tea. Snack or full meal, the choice is yours in the delightful restaurant, which is fully licensed and offers both indoor and outdoor facilities. The varied menu includes Jersey Cream Teas, home-made pastries, sandwiches and a wide selection of locally grown produce on the help-yourself salad bar. On display inside the building you can see the original car used in the Bergerac TV series and every visitor has the FREE chance to win a fabulous car, just fill in an entry form when you visit. Also offering facilities for nursing mothers and the disabled, Jersey Goldsmith can

FAMOUS JERSEYMEN AND WOMEN

As might be expected, Jersey has produced several keen sailors and explorers who took to the seas to begin new lives. Two such men, John Cabot and Philip Langlois, moved to Salem, Massachusetts, the town known the world over for its famous witch trials. Cabot was born in St Helier in 1680 and moved to America in 1700 where he established himself as a merchant. Resourceful and intelligent, he founded the Cabot family of America of whom it is said "The Lowells speak only to Cabots, But the Cabots speak only to God."

Born in Trinity, Philip Langlois, another merchant, changed his name to English on reaching the New World and, at one time, had 27 ships in his fleet; two of which traded solely between Salem and Jersey. He also played an important part in bringing boys and girls over to Salem where they were indentured to tradesmen and given a good education and other opportunities that would not ordinarily have come their way on the Island.

Lillie Langtry, born Lillie Le Breton, married Edward Langtry at St Saviour's Church in 1874. The couple moved to London and Lillie became the toast of London society, gaining her nickname 'Jersey Lily' as much for her beauty as for her considerable charm and intelligence. It is another Le Breton, Philip Hemery Le Breton, that the people of London thank for the preservation of Hampstead Heath in the mid 1800s.

The famous artists, John Everett Millais, born in Southampton in 1829, moved to Jersey with his family in 1833. A child prodigy, Millais was accepted as a student at the Royal Academy in 1840. His best known works include a portait of Lillie Langtry painted in 1878.

Victor Hugo the French novelist and political activist, lived on St Clement's Coast Road though he was expelled in 1855, after supporting three friends who were said to have insulted Queen Victoria, and moved to Guernsey.

Today the island is home to Jack Higgins, author of *The Eagle has Landed*, John Nettles best known for his television role as Bergerac, which is also filmed on the Island, Derek Warwick, the Grand Prix racing driver and globe-trotting Alan Whicker.

keep a whole family entertained for hours and is open from 10 am onwards.

To the south and right on the shore of the Bay, **Kempt Tower** was another of the Island's defences built during the Napoleonic Wars. Today, the Tower is an information centre with exhibitions and displays on the flora and fauna of the area. Some of the best views of St Ouen's Bay can be had from the top of the tower.

Also known as La Mare au Seigneur, **St Ouen's Pond** is the largest natural stretch of freshwater in the Channel Islands. Originally only separated from the Bay by a narrow shingle bank, during the Occupation the Germans built two canals, at either end, and filled them full of traps in case of an invasion by the Allies. St Ouen's Pond lies at the heart of the Les Mielles de Morville nature reserve.

Situated above L'Etacq overlooking the magnificent St Ouen's Bay, **Fine Gems and Craft Centre** adds an extra sparkle to your holiday. When choosing a diamond or any other type of jewellery - value, quality and confidence is all important, so you will be pleased to know there are friendly well trained staff always available to help and advise you. Diamonds of the same size, at a glance can look alike, but in truth they can be very different, so expert advice is a must. You can watch the craftsmen create, set and adjust items to suit your personal taste and for added interest there is a small working pottery and gift shop.

Fine Gems and Craft Centre

During your visit you can view the largest selection of diamonds in the Channel Islands, displays and replicas of famous diamonds including the Crown Jewels.

Within the extensive displays and showroom is the licensed Potters tearoom and Diamond Patio offering delicious refreshments and light lunches. Fine Gems also has an extensive open grassed area, where you can sit and admire the view or freedom for the children to play while you enjoy an afternoon tea or a bite to eat. This sparkling attraction with its spectacular views, offers you the best value on the Island with prices that are guaranteed VAT free and a selection that is second to none.

Fine Gems and Craft Centre, Les Landes, St Ouen
Tel: 01534 483755

Situated overlooking St Ouen's bay is one of Jersey's most popular hotel and restaurants. **The Lobster Pot** is housed in a 17th century granite farmhouse (though this is no ordinary farmhouse) nestled between cliffs on the northwest coast. The standard of service is as one would expect of an exclusive establishment. Under the direction of Michelin award winning Chef du Cuisine Mr Kevin John Broome and his wife Lisbeth, the Hotel and Restaurant team ensure their guests' every need is catered for. A smooth start is guaranteed by arranging your transfer from the airport to the Hotel, either by Hotel courier or hire car. The Hotel staff are always happy to advise and recommend visitors of the best sights to see. For the energetic, mountain bikes are provided at no extra cost, enabling guests to explore the Island in the traditional way.

The Lobster Pot

The Hotel has twelve rooms, all created with warmth and comfort in mind. The individual furnishings illustrate the personal touch of a small luxurious hotel. All rooms have their own remote control television with Fastext and Sky, video recorder, music centre, direct dial telephone and personal fax machine. In addition to these facilities, the hotel also provides an in-house entertainments library. With a twenty four hour room service, you needn't even leave your room to enjoy the tastes of the

Grosnez Castle

restaurant.

Breakfast in the restaurant should not be missed in order to begin the day with warmth and flavour. You will be greeted with fresh museli, home-made pancakes and orange syrup, freshly ground coffee and a variety of freshly infused teas. Alternatively, sample the great British Breakfast. The menu at lunch and supper specialises in seafood, one of Jersey's most traditional foods. Market fresh lobsters, crawfish, sea bass, langoustines and local oysters are cooked to resemble a variety of world cuisines. Also on offer in the Bistro Broome is a large menu of vegetarian and meat dishes and of course a delicious selection of puddings to round off your meal. Children are catered for in the same style with their own à la carte and exclusive drinks menu to choose from, with a surprise at the end. Exclusive to The Lobster Pot is the Chef's private dining room where serious food is served. Both dishes from the past and dishes of the future can be savoured as well as excellent Vintage wines and house Champagne. Both hotel and restaurant are kept simple, a solution Kevin John Broome believes is the closest answer to perfection.

The Lobster Pot - Kevin John Broome Hotel & Restaurant, L'Etacq, St Ouen Tel: 01534 482888 Fax: 01534 481574

GROSNEZ POINT

As might be supposed, the name Grosnez does not come from the French for 'big nose' but is derived from the Viking 'gras ness' meaning grey headland. The mysterious ruins of **Grosnez Castle** lie on the Point, the northwest promontory of Jersey. Probably built in the 14th century, by 1540 it was described as a ruin on Popinjay's map. As the Castle had no well it is unlikely that it was ever used as a garrison but it may have been built as a place of refuge. It was probably deliberately demolished in 1468 when the Island was recaptured from the French.

To the south of the headland lies a rock known as **Le Pinacle** which has featured as an object of worship and as a ceremonial site for many thousands of years. Evidence found here suggests that Neolithic man used the rock and four other periods of history are also represented; a copper axe from the Copper Age, a Bronze Age spearhead, an Iron Age settlement and, finally, Roman coins. For those with less interest in history and more interest in flora, the main glory is the blaze of colour provided by the wild flowers found growing here.

The flat heathland of the **Les Landes** area, found on this northwestern corner of Jersey, makes it an ideal location for **Les Landes Racecourse** which holds race meetings throughout the summer months.

LA GREVE DE LECQ

The name literally means beach of Lecq and, in 1215, it was spelt La Wik, which leads to the belief that the name may have been derived from the old Norse word vik (meaning bay). However, Lecq may also have come from an old Breton word meaning stone or rock though the stones found on the beach actually come from the breaking up of the harbour. Whatever the derivation of the name, La Grève de Lecq is steeped in history.

To the east of the Bay, can be seen the high conical hill that was once an Iron Age fortification and the Grève de Lecq Inn was once a mill that was first mentioned in 1551. The **Barracks** here are the last surviving on the Island. Built around 1810 there was a separate block for officers and numerous buildings for stores and stables. Now owned by the National Trust the Barracks is popular with visitors in the summer and has an information centre.

Hotel Des Pierres

A warm welcome awaits you at the family run **Hotel Des Pierres**, situated only a few yards from the shore of the beautiful north coast bay of La Grève de Lecq, this attractive Hotel has a location that is simply perfect. Within walking distance of some of the best bathing beaches in Jersey, breathtaking coastal walks, countryside and historical sites, Des Pierres is at the very gateway of Jersey. The Hotel has been awarded three diamonds which is a seal of approval given by the Island's Tourism Authority, and it is highly acclaimed by the RAC and AA Selected QQQQ. All of the 16 en-suite bedrooms have colour TV, radio, tea and coffee making facilities and central heating, and all boast a view of either the sea and coast or green woodlands.

The Des Pierres prides itself on an excellent reputation for the finest cuisine and a comprehensive menu that will impress even the most travelled gourmet. There is a choice of twelve different breakfasts in the mornings and a full vegetarian menu is offered at all sit down meals. The cocktail bar lounge has a nautical atmosphere and stocks a wide range of beers, wines and spirits all at inexpensive Jersey prices. There is also a separate TV lounge, a mini gym with free weights where you can keep in shape and some picturesque gardens where you can just sit and enjoy the spectacular view.

On the doorstep of Des Pierres is La Grève de Lecq, an old smuggling harbour with a large sandy beach where swimming is a pleasure at all states of the tide, and a favourite spot for local anglers. Around from the headland are cliff paths where you are surrounded by the scent of wild flowers and caves waiting to be found. Why not hire cycles from the Hotel and explore the inland through leafy country lanes, woodland and farms where each field has its own name and an abundance of flowers and wildlife. Within a mile there is a shire horse farm, a pottery, vineyard, rifle range, a butterfly farm, candlecraft and riding stables, so you can never say that you are bored with this array of entertainment. There are also the luxury boutiques, restaurants, night clubs and duty free shops to explore in St Helier and all can be enjoyed by using the bus route which is just five miles from town.

Hotel Des Pierres, La Grève de Lecq Bay
Tel: 01534 481858 Fax: 01534 485273

ST MARY'S VILLAGE

First mentioned in 1042, **St Mary's Church** was described around that time as Ecclesia Ancte Marie arsi monasterii, St Mary of the Burnt Monastery. The site of the monastery is not known but it is likely that it once stood where the parish church was later rebuilt. The present Church dates back to Norman times and the oldest part to still be seen is the northeast chancel where the remains of two round headed Norman windows are visible. One of the more interesting relics here is a priest's tombstone which lies sideways in the outside of the west wall; it shows a man with a chalice and fish on either side, these being the emblems of Christianity. Traditionally, on Christmas Eve the church bell is rung and carries on ringing for a full 24 hours. This is believed to have originated during the times of the Norman occupation of the Island in 1461-8 and the practice is carried out less whole-heartedly throughout the neighbouring parishes.

Centred on an attractive 18th century farmhouse **La Mare Vineyards** are the only commercial vineyards on the Island. Open to the public between April and October (Monday to Saturday), there are wine tastings and children are welcome to play in the orchards.

The **Jersey Flower Centre** is the home of the 'Flying Flowers', a mail order operation that sends flowers all over the world. Set in beautiful surroundings, to the southeast of St Mary's Village, as well as the flowers, there is plenty to see and do at the centre. Wildfowl and exotic birds live in the grounds, which can be discovered by following the specially constructed pathways, and visitors can also see exactly what it takes to become the world's largest flower mail order operation. A video presentation gives the history of the company and the progress of the flowers as they are cut, graded and packed can also be watched. The Visitor Centre, which incorporates a licensed restaurant and gift shop is open from April to October.

North from St Mary's Village is **Le Col de la Rocque**, a National Trust owned headland that provides a wonderful viewpoint. A paradise for flower enthusiasts, there can be found a wide variety of wild plants and flowers including gorse, wild daffodils, bluebells, foxgloves and blackberries, all thriving on the thin headland soil. Off the coast of St Mary, is a small islet, **L'Ile Agois** that was once the home to early Christian hermits. Now belonging to the National Trust, the islet is only approachable at low tide but within living memory there was a plank bridge connecting it to the mainland.

ST JOHN

Though a small parish, St John's has some of the finest scenery on the Island. From its coast, on a clear day, can be seen Alderney and the coast of France while most often Guernsey and Sark can be viewed. Inland it is agriculture that dominates the landscape and the fields are given over to grazing for the famous Jersey cows. Also inland lies the tumulus of **La Hougue Boëte**, which dates from around 3500 BC.

The northern coastal road, **Route de Nord**, was built during the German Occupation and gave much needed work to those Islanders who were determined not to work for the enemy. It is to those men and women that the road is dedicated. Dedicated to St John the Baptist, the **Parish Church** was first mentioned in 1150. The oldest part of the present church is the north chancel though many additions and alterations have been made over the years.

Situated in the parish of St John on La Route du Nord, **Les Fontaines Tavern** boasts some spectacular views out over the Atlantic Ocean. The name Les Fontaines arises from the fact that there were underground springs in this area and the water used in the small waterfall display at the Inn comes from a 90 foot deep bore. The original building was once a 15th century farmhouse and the cider press on the property was still in use up until the last war.

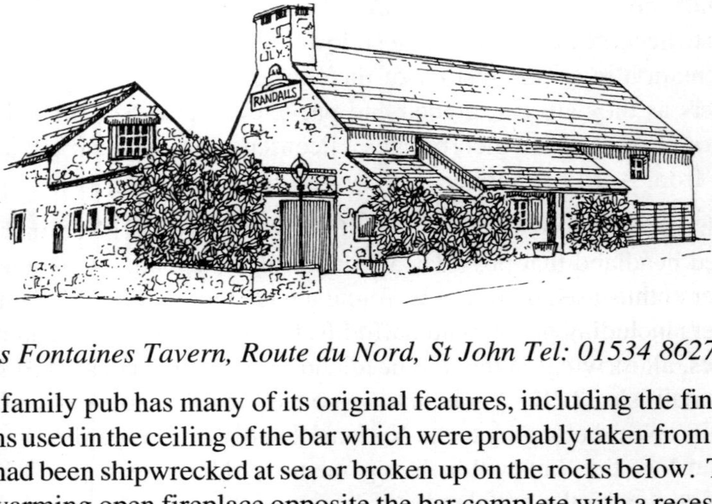

Les Fontaines Tavern, Route du Nord, St John Tel: 01534 862707

This family pub has many of its original features, including the fine oak beams used in the ceiling of the bar which were probably taken from ships that had been shipwrecked at sea or broken up on the rocks below. There is a warming open fireplace opposite the bar complete with a recess that would have once been used for baking and cooking purposes. Les

Fontaines was enlarged by the addition of a new lounge which has continued the granite theme of the inn and to the rear of the Tavern there is a building that was once used as a private school. In 1965 the premises were purchased by the Hon EG Greenall for Randall's Brewery and the Tavern has been very capably managed by Georgina Berresford for the passed two years.

ST LAWRENCE

The parish is rich in old buildings, both large and small, and perhaps one of the most mellow on the Island is the 17th century **La Ferme Morel**. A typical farmhouse, now belonging to the National Trust of Jersey, it retains its cider press and crusher. Also of note is the **Hamptonne Country Life Museum**; comprising a rural, medieval dwelling, 17th century house, and early 19th century farmhouse with some Victorian outbuildings that is well worth a visit. Actors lead visitors through the rooms where they can try out the furniture and also visit a working cider press and apple crusher. On Sunday afternoons there are a series of special events where visitors can listen to an 18th century Methodist preacher or to musicians from the late 18th century talking about their views on life. Open daily between March and October, there is always something special to see here.

It is very likely that the nave, tower and transept of **St Lawrence's Church** date from before 1198 when the first mention of the church was made. During restoration of the church in 1892 a broken granite pillar of non-Jersey stone was uncovered which bears the inscription " UD DI LAU SER RIGON D". The pillar obviously came from a Roman villa of about the 3rd or 4th century but the inscription was added later, in the 6th century. The meaning has been debated over the years and it is probable that is it represents the name of the priest and his origin and so most likely means "Lau, from Rigond, Servant of God".

For the people of Jersey, the Second World War was a unique and harrowing experience for, during five long years, Jersey and the other Channel Islands were the only British soil to be invaded and occupied by German forces, and the most ruthless military machine the world has ever seen has left its indelible mark on the quiet countryside. A chill is apparent within moments of entering the echoing entrance tunnel of the **German Underground Hospital**. This is no fabrication, no late 20th century theme park fantasy. This is the real thing. Hewn in human misery. Within yards of the entrance is a section of bare, splintered rock face where a simple plaque records: "Under these conditions men of many nations laboured to construct this hospital. Those who survived will never forget; those who did not will never be forgotten."

The kilometre-long tunnels and galleries were clawed out of brittle shale with gunpowder and handtools and then clad in 6,000 tonnes of concrete as hundreds of forced labourers toiled like ants in an underground hell. Careful reconstruction of many of the areas within the Hospital - the operating theatre, doctors and nurses' quarters, wards, offices, stores and several unfinished tunnels - bring to life, with chilling realism, the experience of those who suffered appalling hardships to build tunnels, and the subterranean twilight lives of those it was constructed for.

German Underground Museum, Meadowbank, St Lawrence

Rare wartime archive film and a compelling collection of Occupation artifacts displayed in a unique environment bring the experience of thousands of Islanders caught up in war, vividly to life. Opened in 1995, within the Underground Hospital, a special exhibition titled *A year in the life...*, commemorates the 50th anniversary of the Island's liberation. The Miere Collection comprises memorabilia assembled by retired curator Joe Miere - who as a teenager was imprisoned by the German secret police for acts of terrorism against the occupying forces. Together these exhibitions poignantly highlight the drama and tragedy of an Island people torn out of their peaceful existence, flung into the turmoil of world war and face-to-face with an enemy literally at the door and who experienced invasion, occupation and eventually joyful liberation.

The German Underground Hospital and adjacent Sanctuary Visitor Centre and Restaurant are at Meadowbank, St Lawrence, and are open daily from mid-March until mid-November from 9.30 am until last admission at 4.15 pm and from mid-November until mid-March (excluding January) on Sunday and Thursday afternoons.

Hotel Cristina

Occupying an elevated position in the very centre of St Aubin's Bay, **The Hotel Cristina** boasts panoramic views over the sandy beach and the attractive Coronation Park. The setting is particularly delightful as the Hotel is surrounded by well tended flower filled terraced gardens at various levels. This choice site has been habited by humans for thousands of years, the remains of a Neolithic man were found within the original grounds and in more recent times the hotel was occupied by the German Forces during World War II. The Cristina offers all its guests a high standard of accommodation with all 62 guest rooms having private facilities with bath and shower, colour TV, radio, complimentary tea and coffee tray, hair dryer and direct dial telephone.

All rooms have been tastefully decorated and furnished, with central heating throughout and most bedrooms have a sea view and private balcony. The Hotel Cristina also offers suites, each being equipped to the same high standard as the bedrooms, with the addition of a comfortable lounge including a sleeper settee, suitable for an extra person. The apartments have the same amenities as the suites, but with the added advantage of a separate kitchen.

The Terrace Dining Room and the flower filled balcony with its intimate alcoves, offer magnificent views over St Aubin's Bay and Elizabeth Castle, and in the evenings under the gentle lighting, this is truly a most romantic setting. The newly redecorated restaurant complex is on two levels, with special lighting and dance floor, where evening entertainment is arranged several nights each week from May to September. The pool terrace enjoys a southerly aspect and is a natural suntrap, perfect for relaxing on a sun bed after a dip in the freshwater pool, or enjoying an exotic cocktail from the Dolphin Pool Bar. The Hotel is open to non-residents for lunches and in the evenings for dinner dances, with gentlemen normally wearing jackets for dinner. Being only one and a half miles away from the town of St Helier, Hotel Cristina is the perfect location from which to explore the picturesque harbours and magnificent scenery that Jersey has to offer.

Hotel Cristina, St Lawrence Tel: 01534 58024 Fax: 01534 58028

BEAUMONT

Situated on the Rue de le Halve, which lies on the coast road between St Helier and St Aubin, **The Goose On The Green** is a Randalls Brewery owned Inn that has been managed by your host Angela Capels for the past two years. The exterior is clean and crisp with the windows and skirting being picked out in an attractive deep blue, there are also several traditional Victorian style gas lamps adorning the walls. Open seven days a week for food between 12 pm until 2.25 pm and from 6 pm until 9 pm, the Pub offers its visitors a variety of good home-cooked food at very reasonable prices. At the rear of the Inn there is a pleasant Beer garden complete with children's playground for when the weather is good, but if it is inclement, all are welcome inside the warm and cosy bar area. From

Friday through to Saturday, The Goose on the Green has live bands playing every evening and on Wednesday nights there is a Quiz night, where locals and visitors alike, pit their wits to try and win the top prize. Also to the rear of the Inn is a light and airy conservatory which proves very popular with guests on those sunny days, the perfect place to sit and enjoy a drink or a meal whilst watching the world go by.

The Goose on the Green

Le Moulin de Quétivel

CHAPTER TWO
GUERNSEY

German Bunkers

2
GUERNSEY

Introduction

Guernsey enjoys many similarities with its neighbour Jersey, but it is also very different. Self-governing and with few restricting taxes like Jersey, in Guernsey the public telephone booths are a different colour, the police wear different helmets, the dialect is different and the bailiffs wear different robes. Probably the most important difference between the two islands is that their two breeds of cattle; the Guernsey cow is red and white in colour with a narrow head, a long straight muzzle and a pink nose, while the Jersey, by contrast, is fawn and white with a dish shaped head, a black nose and is slightly smaller in size.

Known as the Green Island, Guernsey is about 25 square miles in size and has many attractive beaches, sandy bays and high cliffs. Inland, there are small farms, mellow farmhouses and red granite churches. It is often said that whilst the new money heads for Jersey, the old money makes for Guernsey. True or not, the Island has a gentle charm all its own that certainly draws people here time and time again.

Finally, the Bailiwick of Guernsey also includes Sark, Alderney and Herm. However, Guernsey, Sark and Alderney each have a different flag though they are all based around the Cross of St George.

Around Guernsey

ST PETER PORT

This is the most ancient town in all the Channel Islands and, with its narrow cobbled streets and Regency and Victorian buildings, it is also one of the most charming. Originally a fishing village, the building of Castle Cornet turned St Peter Port into the Island's main port and two small piers enclose the sheltered harbour. From as far back as the 14th century St Peter Port was a tax free town and imported wines from Bordeaux sending them on to England. This led to smuggling, though the Guerns called it free trade, and this in turn created much of the wealth seen in the town today.

The original **Harbour** piers, Victoria and Albert, eventually became too small to take steamships and, in 1853, Castle Pier was built. St Julian's Pier, built around 1859, completed the formation of the harbour as seen today. On this jetty is a memorial plaque to 33 islanders killed in a German air raid in 1940.

Dominating the harbour entrance is **Castle Cornet**, built in 1206 by Pierre de Préaux, the Governor of Rouen who moved to Guernsey. It was just completed in time for a French raid in 1214 and, by 1244, it had eight towers. Following the seizure of Guernsey, Sark and Alderney by the Marshal of France, Edward III began, in 1340, to recapture the islands, taking all but the Castle which held out for Philip VI for another five years. Extended and reinforced during the Elizabethan age, Castle Cornet remained a Royalist stronghold during the Civil War, only surrendering in 1651. Having seen military action and occupation for over 900 years, the small additions made by the German Occupation forces this century have not made much of an impact on the building. Today, the Castle is open to the public and houses several museums.

The **Royal Guernsey Militia Museum** exhibits the memorabilia of this force from 1743 and lists of Guernsey's governors from 1177. Pride of place in the Museum is given to the sword of Major General Thomas Dundas who strengthened the Island's defences in anticipation of France's declaration of war against England in 1793. Covering military and naval history from the 16th century to the time of the German Occupation, the **Main Guard Museum** also has amongst its collection the Guernsey Falcon, a six pound cannon that was cast in 1550. Whilst the **Maritime Museum** concerns its self with the sea and includes a Gallo-Roman boat and memorabilia from the Royal National Lifeboat Institution.

As well as seeing the paintings in the **Hatton Gallery**, visitors to the Castle can tour the **201 Squadron Museum** (dedicated to the Island's own RAF Squadron) and, finally, **The Armoury**, with its displays of weapons from the time of the Civil War to the present day. Finally, Castle Cornet also incorporates the Island's first jail, its jailer being known as Portier du Château. As the Castle was situated on a tiny islet and the jailer

The Guernsey Falcon at Castle Cornet

lived in the town, during stormy weather he could not make the crossing. As a result there were many escapes, from sheer necessity, as the prisoners were left without food. A new prison was built, on the mainland, between 1811 and 1815. The Castle ceased to be of military use after the Second World War and soon afterwards the ancient tradition of firing a midday gun was reintroduced. It is now one of Guernsey's major attractions.

Known as the Cathedral of the Channel Islands, **St Peter's Church** has grown over the centuries. Originally built of wood, probably in around 1048, what remains today is the 12th century chancel and the south chapel of 1462. The spire was restored in 1721 and the glass is modern, replacing the windows that were blown out during the German Occupation.

To commemorate Queen Victoria's visit to the Island in 1846 **Victoria Tower** was built (in 1848). It served for many years as a signalling station to Alderney.

None of the six town gates reputedly erected by Edward III survive but, in 1700, granite boulders were placed where the gates once stood. As well as acting as a defence for the town, the gates marked the boundary between town and country. This distinction was of great significance as, in rural areas the law of primogeniture applied (the firstborn son inheriting the family lands intact), though it did not apply in the town. The law was finally abolished in 1954.

The home of Victor Hugo between 1856 and 1870, following his expulsion from Jersey, **Hauteville House** is Guernsey's most popular attraction. Choosing Guernsey as his home because Juliette Drouet, his mistress, already lived here, it was during his time here that Hugo wrote his best known work in Britain, *Les Misérables*. Also whilst here he set about decorating and furnishing the house in an elaborate style that has been preserved for today's visitors. Hauteville House is open to visitors between April and September.

Standing on a hilltop overlooking the town, **Fort George** was begun in 1780 as a replacement of Castle Cornet. The Germans armed the Fort and it was destroyed by Allied bombing prior to the Normandy landings. Following the end of the Second World War, the land was sold to a developer and the luxury homes that now give it its name of **Millionaires' Row** were built. **La Vallette Underground Military Museum** housed in a German built tunnel displays relics from 1914 to 1945.

The **Guernsey Aquarium**, as the tunnel is known, has been housed in La Vallette tunnel for 26 years. It was constructed in 1861 in order that the road running along La Vallette might be extended along the base of the cliffs in the direction of Fermain Bay. The plan did not fully materialise and the tunnel served only as an approach to Soldiers Bay. It has had various owners, and is presently owned by David and Anne Miller, both very keen aquarists.

There are currently 47 separate displays, ranging from local sea fish to European freshwater fish and finally to tropical marine fishes, anemones and inverts of various kinds. Also on display can be found frogs, toads, terrapins and basalisks, the resident lizards. The local marine fishes, which are fed twice a week, are on a diet of squid, beef heart, sandeel, and sometimes sprat. The tropical marine and tropical freshwater fish are also fed on a similar diet. The Guernsey Aquarium is an interesting place to visit even if you don't have an aquarium or pond life at home. David and Anne are pleased to help and advise visitors on what to buy for their environment. Open all year round except Christmas Day and New Year's Day.

Guernsey Aquarium, La Vallette, St Peter Port Tel: 01481 723301

Nello Ciotti's **Da Nello's Restaurant** offers a mixture of ambience, character, style and excellent cuisine which has made it one of the Island's most popular venues for the past eighteen years. The building, once a 15th century fisherman's cottage, displays a great deal of character combined with elegant Italian touches. Low beamed ceilings, granite walls and cosy recesses are complemented by stylish wrought iron and leather furniture in the bar. The main restaurant is cosy and heavily beamed, while the conservatory area brims with flowers and greenery for those who like an al fresco atmosphere. Linger in the comfortable bar with a pre-meal drink - a house cocktail or a glass of Champagne, perhaps. Nello himself is always there ensuring the kind of friendly, efficient personal attention which makes all the difference.

Da Nello's Restaurant

His head chef and junior partner is Tim Vidamour, whose innovative style of cooking is both healthy and delicious. He selects quality produce and fresh herbs and uses virgin olive oil for his Mediterranean signature dishes. Chargrilled dishes are a speciality and the blackboard lists the fresh fish and seafood of the day, as well as game in season and other specialities. The à la carte and table d'hôte menus also feature a choice of traditional pastas - linguini with crab and dill is a favourite - and meat dishes such as fillet of beef Italiana, filled with mozzarella and Parma ham, cooked with Marsala wine; and medallions of beef Barola, which are marinated in brandy and herbs, then cooked in red wine and cream. Da Nello's is open for lunch from noon until 2 pm and for dinner from 6.30 pm to 10.30 pm. Egon Ronay Recommended. Worth booking in advance.

Da Nello's Restaurant, 46 Le Pollet, St Peter Port
Tel: 01481 721552 Fax: 01481 724235

FRENCH INFLUENCE

The history of the Channels Islands, along with their geographical position (in the Gulf of St Malo, not the English Channel), has lead to their interesting and unique cultural identity. During his 16 year exile on the Islands, Victor Hugo described them as "pieces of France which fell into the sea and were gathered up by England" and many see the Channel Islands as an "English-speaking province of France".

The Gallic influence is all around; the telephone directories on the islands are littered with names such as de Carteret and de Veulle, descendants of the knights that were rewarded by William, Duke of Normandy for their loyalty after the Norman Conquest of England in 1066. Indeed, to this day the Queen of England is toasted as "Our Duke of Normandy".

A stroll through any town or village will reveal street names such as Rouge Bouillon (Red Spring) and Colomberie (Dovecot), the placenames themselves are often French and, in the bakery windows can be seen croissants and the typical long thin French baguettes.

Each island too has its own language or dialect, a type of Norman-French known as patois. Unfortunately, the use of the dialects is decreasing and is usually spoken by older generations. The patois on Alderney has, however, completely gone; already in decline before the Second World War, the evacuation of the Island killed the language.

The Norman origins of the islanders has also had an important part to play in the development of their cuisine. Isolated from Britain and often not on friendly terms with France, the islanders have also had to fend for themselves and rely on their own ability to provide for their needs. Over the years this has produced a unique style and taste, though parallels with the regional cuisine of Normandy, France can still be seen, that is quiet different from the traditional dishes of the British mainland. However, the excellence of the cuisine all over the Channel Islands is something that can often only be found in the most expensive establishments on the mainland.

Situated on The Quay at St Peter Port, **The Steak and Stilton Restaurant** enjoys a superb position overlooking the harbour and castle. Although the crisp white building looks quite modern, its origins are believed to be circa 1700. First opened as a restaurant in 1963, Mr Crispini has owned the business since 1985. His family name can be traced back to the 1500s when his family in Florence were administrators to the Pope.

The Steak and Stilton

In its early days, the Steak and Stilton Restaurant specialised in serving mainly steak meals, but during his 11 years as proprietor, Mr Crispini has widened the scope of his cuisine to embrace many different types of food. Call in at any time of the day for either a carefully prepared light snack or main meal. For a small cost you can choose from a variety of salads, baguette sandwiches, pasta or spicy specialities. The main menu choice is considerable with a huge selection of hot and cold appetisers and main course choices including fresh fish and seafood dishes, grills, roast duck and chicken dishes, and salads. Meals are served throughout the day the quality of which is excellent.

The Steak and Stilton, The Quay, St Peter Port
Tel: 01481 723080

Jill's Coffee Shop is approached by the North Esplanade and is also found by passing through Le Pollet Pharmacy to the lower floor level. The building was once an old barrel store in the 1800s at which time there was only the beach in front. This is a well established business and Jill's menu offers home-cooked food with the emphasis on healthy eating - no fried food here!

Jill's Coffee Shop

Vegetarians will find a good choice and the salad bar is reckoned to be the best on the Island. So call in for morning coffee and see the extensive menu and home-made cakes and gateaux - well worth a visit! A small smoking area is available. Open 8.30 am to 4 pm.

Jill's Coffee Shop, North Esplanade, St Peter Port
Tel: 01481 711021

If you are looking for a sea food restaurant with a difference then look no further than **Vina's Restaurant**, situated just behind the North Esplanade in the heart of St Peter Port. Recently refurbished, with Portuguese terracota decorations predominating, Vina Da Silva, the owner, has 20 years experience in the restaurant trade and you can be sure of a wonderful meal in warm and friendly surroundings. Open daily, Monday to Saturday, Vina's offers a mouth-watering menu of Italian and Continental dishes with plenty of local sea food. There is an ever changing daily specials board and a childrens' menu so everyone is sure to be spoilt for choice. Popular with locals and visitors alike, come early and savour an aperitif in the bar while choosing your meal.

Vina's Restaurant, 44 Lower Pollet Street, St Peter Port
Tel: 01481 723246

Just ten minutes walk from the town of St Peter Port is the **Grange Lodge Hotel**. An impressive looking building akin to a small stately home in appearance. It is thought to have been built as a private house in about 1815 using the profits made from privateering. It stayed in the same hands until purchased by the Mansell family in the 1930s. From this time it has been run as an hotel apart from a five year break during the German Occupation.

Over the years, the Hotel has had many alterations and additions not least of which has been the provision of full en-suite facilities to all 31 bedrooms, the building of self-catering flats as a complex within the extensive grounds of the Hotel and a heated outdoor swimming pool. Despite the changes, the Hotel has retained most of its original features and character. The bedrooms have all the up to date amenities including television, telephone and hospitality tray.

Residents will find a most comfortable lounge and reading room and, of course, a licensed bar and very pleasant restaurant. Guests booking the self-catering flats have full use of the Hotel's recreational and catering facilities. Fully inclusive holidays are available. Awarded 3 Crowns by the Tourist Board.

Grange Lodge Hotel, The Grange, St Peter Port
Tel: 01481 725161 Fax: 01481 724211

ST SAMPSON

The Island's oldest Parish Church stands on the spot where St Sampson landed in around 550 when he arrived to begin his mission to preach. The oldest surviving parts of **St Sampson's Church** are the nave and chancel which were complete by 1350.

In the churchyard can be found the gravestone of Thomas Falla who was killed in 1799 by a 26 pound cannonball "lodged between the main and secondary bones of his thigh".

The Harbour here is an extension of a flooded inlet and part of the quay at the harbour's head is still known as Bridge Street. John Macadam, experimenting with road building in Ayrshire and Cornwall in the 19th century, found that Guernsey granite was ideal to mix with tar to form tarmacadam. Exports of the granite rose from 12,000 tons to 450,000 per year in only 50 years. The use of asphalt, in the 20th century, which uses limestone, killed the trade in Guernsey granite and St Sampson's harbour now concentrates on small vessel repairs and horticultural export business.

Fryer Tuck's Halfway Cafe is just across from the beach, halfway between St Peter Port and St Sampson. It is a very cleanly presented business run by Julia and Jonathan offering an amazingly large menu at a surprisingly low cost - ideal for feeding a family. Although traditional fish and chips are served, this is by no means a fish and chip shop! There are about 12 variations of breakfast, about 20 options on the lunch and dinner menu including Fillet of Scotch Salmon, freshly roasted half chicken, calamari and scampi. Children have their own menu of favourites plus their own vegetarian menu. Additionally, the choice covers soups, pies, steaks and daily chef's specials. The cafe is licensed, very clean and has parking at the rear. Low cost menu for all the family!

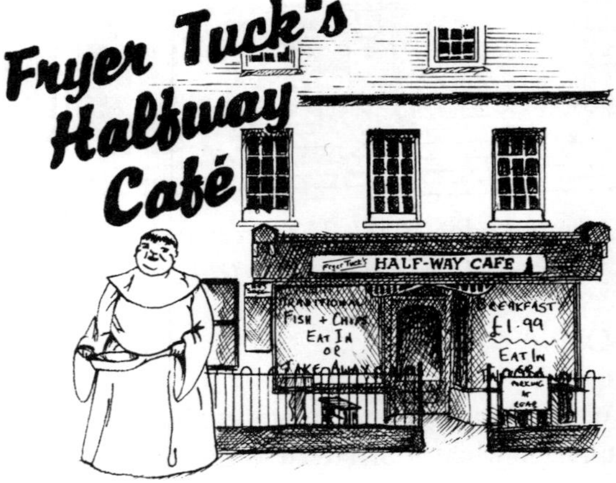

Fryer Tuck's Halfway Cafe, 1 Commercial Place, St Sampsons
Tel: 01481 49448

In the courtyard of the Oatlands Craft Centre is **Ego Motifs**, a small shop with a lot to offer the visitor. You will find a wide selection of beautifully embroidered souvenir jackets, sweatshirts, polo-shirts, T-shirts and caps for both adults and children. Designs include the popular puffin, traditional and modern sailing boats, other designs with a nautical theme, sports, flags, crests, and yacht club burgees, floral Guernsey and other special event designs. Embroidered caps and other woolly hats make a very reasonable present and one size fits all.

All the embroideries are designed and embroidered on the premises by local couple Lynette and Martin Petit. You can see garments being embroidered and, time permitting, can order personalised items from the large range of plain garments, towelling robes and towels, using the stock logos and lettering. Alternatively, specific designs can be made up for both the corporate and leisure market. Mail Order is also possible if your order cannot be completed before you leave.

Ego Motifs, Oatlands Craft Centre, Les Gigands, St Sampson
Tel: 01481 48846 Fax: 01481 42381

BORDEAUX

With a scenic bay, the houses of Bordeaux are as good to look at as the sea. The islets at the northern extremity of the inlet are known as **Les Houmets** and they can be reached at low tide without getting wet. Care however should be take when the tide comes in as the current is dangerous. During the Napoleonic Wars a gun battery was built on Houmet Benest, the closest to the shore, to protect Bordeaux harbour from the north. Though it is not easy to make out its position today, the German gun position close by is clearly visible. The central islet, Houmet Paradis, is also scarred by a German fortification but, before the Second World War, the islet featured in Victor Hugo's novel *The Toilers of the Sea*.

Take a few minutes' walk from the picturesque fishing harbour of Bordeaux and you will arrive at the **Bordeaux Guest House**, a bright white detached house with gardens and a sunny outlook. It has become a home-from-home for business people, shoppers, pilots and visitors from as far afield as Norway and Sweden. Fran and Val, owners of the Bordeaux for the past seven years, offer year-round bed and breakfast accommodation with the option of an evening meal.

Featured in Which? B&B Guide, the Guest House is a popular holiday location for island visitors. The nine guest bedrooms have either en-suite or private bathrooms, all have colour television, radio, intercom, hot drinks facilities and are centrally heated. For the special occasion, book a room with a four poster bed. Fran and Val are great hosts and the relaxed convivial atmosphere in the bar makes for a perfect evening. The lounge is private and has colour television. The home cooking is first class and vegetarian menus and packed lunches are available. A great place to stay and hard to leave!

Bordeaux Guest House, Bordeaux Bay, Vale Tel: 01481 47461
Fax: 01481 43669

L'ANCRESSE

Occupying the northeastern tip of the Island, **L'Ancresse Common** is one of the most visited attractions on Guernsey. As well as having a golf course, many come here to watch the birds and the shipping or just to relax in the sun. The coast line here is littered with defensive structures as the open **L'Ancresse Bay** was very vulnerable to attack. Of those remaining **Fort le Marchant**, standing on Guernsey's most northerly promontory, is well worth a visit. Around **Pembroke Bay**, lies a German anti-tank wall but the very popular broad sands of L'Ancresse beach were not protected by a similar construction.

The Melting Pot restaurant is adjacent to the Pembroke Hotel 100 yards from the beach at Pembroke Bay. Alan and Bettina Earl took over the restaurant a year ago and have given it a completely new look with pastel colours and pine furniture. The new menu has proved very popular with both the local trade and the visitors during the summer months. The interior is light and spacious seating 90 people and the atmosphere is relaxed and informal. The food is a combination of traditional home-cooking and a variety of seafood dishes freshly prepared using local and fresh fish produce. You can choose from the standard table d'hôte or full à la carte menus with the addition of daily specials. The restaurant is open all day during the summer months when cream teas are served and al fresco dining can be enjoyed out of doors. Access is good for wheelchairs and children are welcomed.

The Melting Pot, Pembroke Bay, L'Ancresse, Vale Tel: 01481 41175

VALE

This large parish, second only to Castel is size, was, until the draining of the Braye du Valle, in two parts, separated by the high tide. The Parish **Church of St Michel du Valle** stands on the north shore of the Braye du Valle, overlooking Grand Havre. Situated on a hillock that is only 30 feet above sea level, the surrounding land is so flat that the Church stands out as a landmark. A tombstone, found in the churchyard in 1933, bears markings and inscriptions that date it to the 7th or the 8th century and, along with the dedication of **St Sampson's Church** to a Celtic saint, suggests that there was, in the Dark Ages, a Celtic presence in the north of Guernsey.

As with other medieval churches on the Island, St Michel du Valle has two parallel naves and chancels but the most notable feature of this church is its Romanesque decoration in the south chancel.

In the southern area of the parish, overlooking St Sampson Harbour stands **Vale Castle**, which was as a place of refuge for the islanders

Little Chapel, Vauxbelets

during a time of invasion as well as a defensive structure in this commanding site. In the late 18th and early 19th centuries it was illegal to billet foreign soldiers in England so Russian soldiers who were fighting along side English soldiers in the Netherlands were brought to Vale Castle to rest.

Vale Parish is also home to the Island's finest prehistoric site, **Le Déhus Dolmen**. The dolmen's mound was restored in the 1930s and the side chambers can be explored. Another ancient burial site, **La Varde Dolmen**, is also worth the visit. Though the Germans heavily fortified the hill on which it is found they did not damage the site and there are excellent views from here on a clear day. Close by is **Les Fouillages**, a Neolithic burial chamber is probably unique in western Europe and was excavated in 1978.

COBO

The distinctive red-pink rocks found along the coast here is known as Cobo granite and it has been used extensively in buildings on this side of the Island. Housed in an original manual telephone exchange, the **Telephone Museum**, spans the history of telephone communication on the Island from its humble beginnings in 1898 right up to the present day. Opened in 1976, the Museum is open to the public between April and September on Tuesdays and Wednesdays.

Another larger museum that is well worth a visit is **Guernsey Folk Museum**, founded in 1968 and housed in the former stables of Saumarez Park. It contains collections of agricultural machinery, a recreation of aspects of farming life on the Island a hundred years ago, a Victorian bedroom, kitchen, dairy and wash-house and also a cider barn with a horse-powered apple-crusher. The House here was built in the 18th century and became the home of Admiral Sir James de Saumarez, Nelson's second-in-command during the Napoleonic Wars. During the Second World War it served as the States Offices and is now a retirement home. The **Battle of Flowers** was begun in 1930 and the event is similar to that on Jersey. It is held every August in Saumarez Park.

CASTEL

The correct name for the Parish Church of Castle, Guernsey's largest parish, is **Ste Marie du Câtel**. Legend has it that the Church was built on the site of a Viking fort and this is what gives the parish its name; the position of the Church certainly suggests that it was built on a strategic site. Mentioned in a Papal Decree of 1155, the oldest part of the Church is the western half of the north aisle. As the Church lies on the edge of the parish boundary, Castle had several medieval chapels to serve the outlying districts.

Le Friquet Flower and Butterfly Centre is a working nursery, growing carnations, chrysanthemums and many other varieties, with a butterfly house where both the exotic and the European butterflies fly freely. Fortunately the birdeating spiders are kept in glass cages. Also at the centre is a playground, mini-golf course, radio-controlled boats and a restaurant which make it a great place to visit with all the family. Le Friquet Flower and Butterfly Centre is open between Easter and October.

KING'S MILLS

The village is home to one of the more unusual museums that visitors will ever come across. The **Guernsey Tomato Centre and Museum** tells the story of the tomato, its rise in popularity and its effects on the economy of Guernsey. Greenhouses were first put up on the Island in 1805 to cultivate grapes; it was not until the mid 19th century that tomatoes, having been declared good for the health, were grown here, replacing the vines in most if not all the greenhouses. The industry is now in decline and many growers are turning to plant cultivation. Visitors can also see orchids and pearls here, there is a cartoon cinema and, at the barbecue restaurant, tomato wine can be sampled.

Nearby **Talbot Valley** offers a real opportunity to see rural Guernsey. A stream runs beside the road and once several watermills operated in the vale, though the only one surviving today is at **Les Niaux**, a large overshot waterwheel that is well worth seeing.

The **Fleur du Jardin** is situated in the heart of the delightful conservation village of King's Mills amongst some of the Island's most beautiful rural scenery. Just a short walk from the popular beach of Vazon Bay it is ideally placed for exploring the Island. For those who enjoy country walks, the area around King's Mills is a mass of quiet country lanes heading in all directions.

Strangely the name, Fleur du Jardin, does not come from the literal French translation, flower of the garden, but it is the pedigree name given to the prize winning herd of Guernsey cattle kept here when it was a working farm. This 15th century Inn is steeped in character with exposed beams, thick granite walls, open fires and lovely soft furnishings all coming together to provide a wonderful atmosphere of times gone by. The gardens are full of flowering cherries, shrubs, colourful borders and bright hanging baskets with a heated swimming pool nestling in a quiet part of the garden and kept exclusively for the use of residents. All 17 bedrooms are tastefully furnished and provide quality en-suite accommodation with direct dial telephones, tea and coffee making facilities and hair dryers.

Fleur du Jardin Hotel

The Fleur has always had a resounding reputation for its restaurant and bar meals which are rated amongst the best on the Island, however, with the arrival of their new head chef, who was previously head chef at Keith Floyd's restaurant at Tuckenhay in Devon, the Fleur's reputation has gone from strength to strength and is now worth a significant detour to enjoy a meal at this fine old Inn. There is a constantly changing choice of daily specials with fresh fish and game featuring strongly as well as a good vegetarian selection. All this accompanied by a selection of fine wines, many sold by the glass, well tended Guernsey real ale, and a genuine Guernsey welcome from the ever-friendly staff and you have a really unique place to either stay or enjoy a meal to remember. All inclusive travel and accommodation prices at very competitive rates can be obtained direct from the Fleur du Jardin.

Fleur du Jardin Hotel, King's Mill
Tel: 01481 57996 Fax: 01481 56834

VAZON BAY

The Bay has the largest stretch of sand on the Island and it is a particular favourite with windsurfers. After particularly violent storms, when enough sand has been moved from the beach, the stumps of an ancient drowned forest are revealed. This area was, much earlier, a large peat bog and vazon is Norman French for marsh.

To the north of the Bay, on the headland, stands **Fort Hommet**, one of the three genuine Martello Towers on the Island. It was greatly damaged during the German Occupation and their pill boxes and gun placements can still be seen.

PERELLE

The name comes from the Celtic word meaning rock and, at low tide, the Bay resembles a lunar landscape of rocks. Just inland from Perelle Bay is the **St Apolline's Chapel**, the only surviving medieval chapel on Guernsey. Built towards the end of the 14th century, this tiny chapel (just 27 feet long and 13 feet wide) is dedicated to a deaconess who was burnt alive by the Romans in the 3rd century.

Le Tricoteur have been making guernseys for over a quarter of a century and, over the years, have come to be looked upon as the market leader. Theirs is the only guernsey that is still partly hand knitted and finished entirely in the Island and, although in some cases they may be a little more expensive than the cheaper imported machine-made versions, they represent far better value for money - a proper guernsey will last for years. The original guernsey sweater was knitted by the Island's womenfolk when the Guernseyman still earned his living by working the land and sea. It was, and still is, a supremely practical garment - the hard twist of the wool coupled with close stitching making it surprisingly weather-proof. And, of course, it goes without saying that the guernsey's timeless design make it a fashion classic.

The traditional pattern and knitting skills have been handed down from mother to daughter for centuries, and even today the manufacture of the guernsey is steeped in tradition. To this day, Le Tricoteur guernseys are knitted in the traditional way: by carefully increasing or decreasing the number of stitches in any row, and thereby producing firm selvedges through which wool seaming yarn is sewn. The result is a strong, long lasting garment that will hold its shape better in both wear and washing.

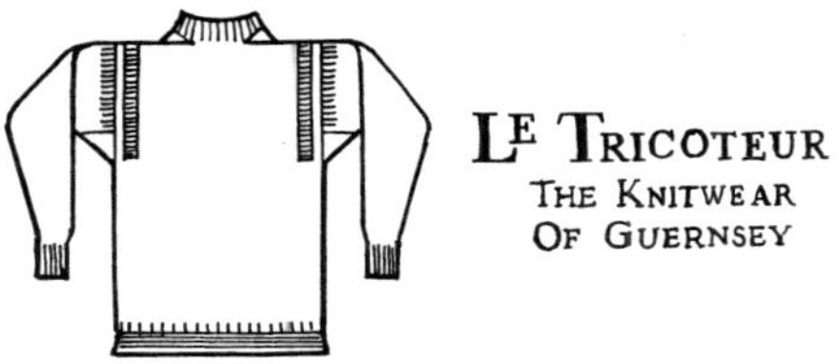

As well as the traditional worsted wool guernsey, Le Tricoteur also make a softer, lighter weight version in pure cotton which, like the woollen version, comes in a wide range of colours and in chest sizes 24 in - 54 in. They also make guernsey jackets, hats, scarves and 'V' necks - all in worsted wool. In recent years, Le Tricoteur have also started knitting in Indigo Denim Cotton that includes cable stitch sweaters, indigo gilets, cardigans and smocks, as well as indigo and ecru stripes. You can visit their factory shop at Perelle which, in addition, has seconds, discontinued lines and factory bargains. It also has a section with some interesting gift items for all ages. Shops are at Perelle Bay and St Peter Port in the Commercial Arcade. They have a world wide mail order service - ask them to put you on their mailing list.

Le Tricoteur, Perelle Bay Tel: 01481 64040 Fax: 01481 64264

L'EREE

This promontory forms the northern arm of Rocquaine Bay and it also overlooks Lihou Island. At one time a place of great importance in pagan worship, Lihou can be reached from L'Erée twice a day at low tide.

Grannie Pauline's Tea Shoppe

On the main L'Erée Coast at St Pierre Du Bois, we discovered **Grannie Pauline's Tea Shoppe** where you can enjoy home-made food and lovely sunsets. Established over 20 years as a tea shop, Grannie Pauline took over the ownership two years ago. The Tea Shop is cleanly presented with newly painted white exterior, whilst inside everything is clean, neat and tidy with a country kitchen style of decor and wooden beams decorated with plants and woven baskets. Light meals and snacks are served throughout the day and the home-made soup and French bread, home-made cakes, luxury ice-creams and special varieties of teas and coffees are particularly recommended. Open in summer 9 am to 6 pm and in winter 10 am until 5 pm.

Grannie Pauline's Tea Shoppe, L'Erée Tel: 01481 63345

ST PETER'S

The Parish's full name is St Pierre du Bois (St Peter in the Wood) and the parish church is known by its French name. Dating from 1375, with 15th century additions, the **Church of St Pierre** has an impressively large tower with 13 bells which give it the largest peal on Guernsey.

Towards the southern end of Rocquaine Bay stands **Fort Grey**, one of Guernsey's true Martello Towers. It was built in 1804 as a defence against invasion by the French but it replaced an early structure, known as Château de Rocquaine, which is believed to have been here from the 17th century. Manned by the British during the First World War and the Germans during the Second, it is now Guernsey's **Maritime Museum**. The emphasis here is on the ships that have been wrecked off the coast, the earliest recorded loss being made in 1309. It was not until **Hanois Lighthouse** was completed in 1862 that sailing these waters became less hazardous. The Museum building, which stands on a little islet, has gained the nickname the Cup and Saucer and it is easy to see why.

The Coach-house Gallery was started in 1975 at Braye du Valle by a group of practising artists and enthusiasts. It has now settled into a permanent home at Les Islets, St Peter's. The sympathetically restored complex of old farm buildings and cottages which, in 1982, received a commendation from the UK Civic Trust for the conversion, provides an attractive setting on two floors with an adjacent etching studio and pottery workshop. There is a monthly change of exhibits. Most work is for sale and ranges from small pieces of pottery, glass and other craftwork to beautiful paintings and sculpture from established visiting artists. Over the years work has been shown by James Butler RA, Vivian Pitchforth RA, Nenne van Dijk and prints by Graham Clarke and Norman

Ackroyd, RE. The directors have a special interest in printmaking and the work of many accomplished artists in this field can always be seen, together with prints and paintings of Guernsey subjects by the gallery artists. The complex is well worth a visit if you enjoy beautiful things. Open all year.

Coach-house Gallery, Les Islets, St Peter's Tel: 01481 65339

FOREST

Also known by its French name, Forêt, the parish has magnificent cliffs and the coastal path has many excellent view points.

Guernsey played as important a role in Hitler's fortification of the Channel Islands as Jersey and the **Occupation Museum**, housed in a low cottage, has amassed a wide ranging collection of memorabilia of that terrifying time. Exhibits include forms, newspapers, documents and permits which all played an important part in the life of the islanders under an occupying force. There is also a large display of weapons and small arms and the recreated Occupation kitchen shows what the islanders were forced to eat in late 1944. The Museum is open daily from April to October and on Sundays, Tuesdays and Thursdays from November to March.

If you are looking for the perfect family holiday, **The Mallard Hotel Complex** is a resort in itself - equally, it is ideal for the single traveller and couples young and old - The Mallard Complex has something for everyone. Close to the Island's best beaches and cliff walks featuring some of the most spectacular views in Europe but it is only a short ride into Guernsey's capital, St Peter Port. The range of facilities on offer at the Mallard encompass just about everything you could wish for; Egon Ronay voted the Mallard 'Best four Crown Hotel in 1994 & 1995' and the management constantly strives to maintain high standards and ensure attentive service from their friendly staff.

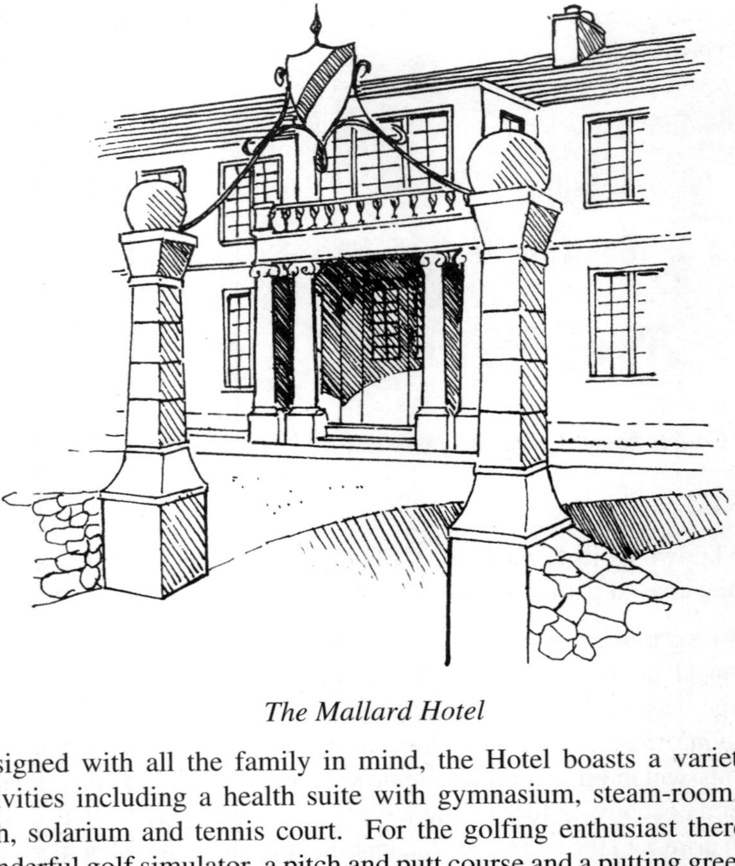

The Mallard Hotel

Designed with all the family in mind, the Hotel boasts a variety of activities including a health suite with gymnasium, steam-room, spa bath, solarium and tennis court. For the golfing enthusiast there's a wonderful golf simulator, a pitch and putt course and a putting green. If you are looking for a more leisurely time then relax in the Diving Duck Bar and listen to live music or savour the chef's award wining cuisine. Each of the 47 bedrooms have private bathrooms satellite TV, tea and coffee making facilities, baby listening service and room service. Some rooms have ground floor locations with two specially equipped for the disabled guest. The Hotel restaurant seats 130 people and serves dinner until 10 pm. The chef provides a superb range of dishes with enough variety to suit most tastes. Ask about special breaks and the many other facilities of the hotel. Impressive by any standards.

The Mallard Hotel, Forest Tel: 01481 64164 Fax: 01481 65732

LE BOURG

The **Church of Ste Marguérite de la Forêt** is thought to have been built on an ancient burial site and, indeed, the oldest parts of the Church rest on a series of boulders which certainly could have been part of a dolmen. With a circular churchyard, which could be describing the shape of a burial mound, there is reasonable evidence to support this theory. Unlike most English churches, where the north doors were used during baptisms (the Devil fleeing from the church as he lost another soul to God), the north door of the Church of Ste Marguérite de la Forêt was used by the women and children; the men used the south door.

VILLIAZE

The **Guernsey Botanical Gardens** opened in 1992 on the site of the Island's zoo and some of the old aviaries are used to house collections of finches and parakeets. Set in splendid grounds, there is information on Guernsey's flora, including its medicinal plants, a children's playground, gift shop and restaurant. The Botanical Gardens are open daily and make an interesting and informative visit.

ST ANDREW

This is the only one of Guernsey's ten parishes that is without a coastline. Near the parish border with St Peter Port is **The Hangman's Inn**, the site, in days gone by, of many executions. One of the better known victims of the gallows which stood here for centuries was Gaultier de la Salle. The exact reason for his fate is unknown but it is thought that he either illegally executed a fellow officer, who had received a Royal Pardon, or he framed a neighbour for theft in order to gain the upper hand in a dispute of a water well.

One of the most chilling reminders of the years of occupation on the Island is the **German Underground Hospital**. The tunnels in which the hospital were built were dug by slave labour and as they died on their feet digging their bodies were thrown into the wet concrete floors and walls. It took some three and a half years to complete the work during which

La Gran'mère du Chimquière

time some 60,000 tons of rock was moved and 1.2 miles of tunnel were created along with 75,000 square feet of floorspace. Originally planned to hold 500 patients the hospital was eventually used to store thousands on tons of ammunition. The hospital provided medical services here for only six weeks, from the time of the Normandy landings until the Allies' advance. This, however, was not a great loss as the patients were deprived of sunlight. Little has altered since the day of liberation and with all the medical equipment removed, the hospital is a sombre and solemn place which is open to the public from April to September.

The **Little Chapel**, at Vauxbelets, is said to be the smallest in the world. It can hold six people comfortably and is based on the grotto and Church of Ste Bernadette at Lourdes. Brother Déodat Antoine, a de la Salle monk built his first tiny chapel in 1914 but destroyed it as soon as he had finished. His second chapel stood until 1923 when he again demolished his work and began the chapel that is seen today. Leaving a fellow brother to finish it, Antoine left for France shortly before the outbreak of the Second World War due to illness. The Little Chapel is decorated, inside and out, with tiny pieces of pottery and china. The large building behind it was the monastery but is now a language school.

Sharing the Little Chapel site is the **Guernsey Clockmakers** where visitors can watch wooden casings for grandfather clocks, wall barometers and other similar objects being made.

The 12th century **Parish Church** is dedicated to St André de la Pommeraye (St Andrew in the Apple Orchard) but its original Latin name was Ecclesia Sancti Andreae de Putente Pomeria, meaning that the orchard was on a gradient. One of the smallest churches on the Island, the apple orchard has now gone but the church does stand on a hill side.

ST MARTIN

By way of a contrast with its neighbour St Andrew's Parish, which has no coastline, this parish has Guernsey's longest stretch of coastline. The Parish **Church of St Martin de la Bellouse** is known for its menhir, **La Gran'mère du Chimquière**, who stands guard by the gate. The human figure carved in granite dates around 2500-1800 BC but the detail on the face was added much later probably by the Romans, 100 BC-AD 100. From the 18th century onwards the statue was the focus of witchcraft and black magic ceremonies.

Housed in the sympathetic surroundings of a Tudor barn on the Sausmarez Manor Estate at St Martin, **The Treasure Chest** is probably the most comprehensive specialist dolls' house and miniature shop in the Channel Islands. This magical world of miniatures will fascinate and enthral you, browse among the houses, kits, furniture and books with friendly and helpful staff always at hand to offer advice and assistance. This unique collection of dolls' houses, some of which date back to the early 1830s, was originally started by Patricia Borwick and established on Lihou Island. Today The Treasure Chest is now owned and run by Richard and Shirley Hardwick and the collection can be viewed daily from 1st March to 1st February from 10 am to 5 pm (Easter to October 10 am to 6 pm). School parties and groups are welcome by prior arrangement and there is ample free parking for all.

The Treasure Chest, Sausmarez Manor Estate, St Martin
Tel: 01481 35904 Fax: 01481 37516

Sausmarez Manor is recommended by Travel Which, in the AA top 20 houses open to the public for 1995 and in the only 21 houses recommended in Britain by the Courvoisier's Book of the Best. The home of the Seigneurs de Sausmarez for nearly a millennium, is one of the longest single ownership properties in Britain. This architectural gem was part created at the bequest of the 1st Governor of New York and is regarded as the finest example of Queen Anne colonial architecture in Britain. The guided tours of the house unfold the changing fortunes of the Island and the family who have been: privateers, explorers, judges, diplomats, cartographers, inventors, sportsmen, admirals, generals and prelates, most of whom have left some mark on the architecture or contents. Open Monday to Thursday at 10.30 am, 11.30 am, 2.00 pm and 3.00 pm during the season (June to September) and in the mornings Easter to May and October.

Nestling in a delightful informal garden with an intriguing wild woodland sub-tropical garden crammed with rare, exotic and the unusual mixed with the more familiar; look out for the collections of camellias (300), hostas, bamboos, cyclamen, fuchsias, bananas and eucalyptus. The Sunday Times, Daily Telegraph and the RHS Magazine - The Garden, have all written about the gardens. The Seigneur's pitch and put is the largest and most congenial on the Island. Whilst there, enjoy a train ride through the wood, a snack at the Egon Ronay Tearoom or visit the delightful Dolls' House Collection in a Tudor barn, and let the children clamber over Scrambly Castle Play Area or simply feed the free range ducks, geese and fowls who instantly make you feel welcome.

Sausmarez Manor

The Happy Hollow Pitch and Put Course was created by the current Seigneur with its bunkers, water hazard and sprinkler system on the lovely greens. It is a challenging course and now that it has been opened for the public to enjoy it is proving very popular with regulars and visitors. Equipment is provided free to enable it to be an inexpensive 40 minutes or so for the experienced and not so experienced. The separate 9 hole putting green is not so serious though the No 8 can try the patience and skill a bit. Open daily during the season and weekends throughout the year.

Sausmarez Manor, St Martin Tel: 01481 35571

An attraction well worth a visit is **Manor Trains Pleasure Centre** at St Martin. Take a ride on a train which meanders on a seven and a quarter inch track for a quarter of a mile moving along at a gentle pace through the woods - a ride enjoyed by young and old (the current record holder being a lady of 93 years). Natural plant life is kept under control whilst teddy bears and other such 'animals' hide amongst the trees. The not so eccentric driver might warn you not to talk to the teddies "cause they'll think you're mad"!

There are also drive-yourself 'G' scale trains to wizz around their own mini garden. Children up to seven years of age can enjoy the free swings and slides and adjacent to the train area is a fortress for the older children. For those in their first or second childhood - this is one to enjoy! Open Easter to October 31st and most weekends in between.

Manor Trains Pleasure Centre, Sausmarez Manor, Sausmarez Road, St Martin Tel: 01481 727286

Tucked away down the wooded lanes of rural St Martin, a few minutes away from picturesque south coast bays and cliffs you'll discover **The Captain's Hotel** with its charming old beamed interior. Although enjoying an ideal privacy, the Hotel is only minutes by car from the centre of St Peter Port. This is a wonderful location for those who enjoy cycling and walking and of course, lounging on the beach.

Run by Alison and Colin de la Mare, who clearly enjoy their work and insist on the best for their customers, the Hotel has a great warmth and it is easy to see why the Hotel and Captain's Bistro is so popular with residents and islanders. Fresh fish is a speciality of the Bistro, supplied by local fishermen. Numerous other interesting dishes are displayed on the chalk boards around the restaurant with several dishes for vegetarians. Chargrilled Ribeye Steak and Fillet of Pork looked a popular choice with diners.

The guest bedrooms have en-suite facilities together with radio alarm, tea and coffee making services, television and central heating. The comfortable lounge bar has low ceilings with original oak beams, and boasts a large collection of brass, copper and parochial memorabilia; a very relaxing ambience in which to enjoy a pint of real ale or other beverage. The Hotel also boasts a large and secluded south facing garden where guests can enjoy the summer sunshine. Graded 2 Crowns by the Tourist Board and listed in CAMRA.

The Captain's Hotel, La Fosse, St Martin Tel: 01481 38990
Fax: 01481 39312

MOULIN HUET BAY

Pronounced 'moo-lan wet', out in the bay stands **Cradle Rock**. Legend has it that three local girls fell asleep on the rock and became cut off from the mainland by the incoming tide. No-one ever saw them again. A chilling tale, but the visitors to the Island should take note of the message the sorry tale tells.

Hotel Bon Port is situated in the midst of Guernsey's most beautiful coastal scenery, boasting spectacular views over Moulin Huet Bay, Petit Port Bay, the famous Peastacks, Saints Bay and Harbour and the Island of Jersey. Hotel Bon Port is ideally centred within the 19 miles of cliff paths which wander from St Peter Port along the majestic cliffs to the rugged Pleinmont Point on the southwest tip of the island. You may walk down to Moulin Huet Beach, very secluded and something really special. The gently sloping private gardens and grounds with superb swimming pool and nine hole pitch and put golf course, afford the most delightful views, seen also from your deluxe bedroom and most points of the Hotel. Bedrooms are beautifully fitted and have private bath and shower en-suite. All the little luxuries are provided including television, telephone, trouser press, hair dryer and hospitality tray. The Hotel also has deluxe rooms with private balconies giving panoramic views of the bays and cliffs. Magnificent superior suites offer a further degree of luxury with private entrance, additional colour television and video in the dining room with a breakfast bar and all the usual facilities.

Hotel Bon Port

After a bracing cliff walk or a days shopping, you can relax or work out in the hotel's Health Suite. The fully equipped gym has an Aerobic Step machine, electronic bicycle and a multi gym. For the less energetic there is a mixed sauna and a cool-off shower. Adjacent to the Health Suite can be found the quiet and restful Atrium, a beautiful enclosure, designed to remove your worries and stress with comfortable seats and a soothing water fountain. Day or night the Renoir View Restaurant is stunning; breakfast can be enjoyed here or in your room. It is also open at lunchtime and in the evening with an extensive à la carte menu. Lunch or bar snacks can be taken either inside or outside on the terraces or by the swimming pool.

As you might expect from Guernsey's only 5 Crown Coast Hotel, the service, quality and presentation are top class. You can enjoy all this luxury at very competitive rates. The Manager, Carlos da Silva will ensure your visit is one to remember and will look forward to your return visit. Not to be missed!

Hotel Bon Port, Moulin Huet Bay, St Martin Tel: 01481 39249
Fax: 01481 39596

JERBOURG POINT

The original **Doyle Column** monument was built here in 1825 but was destroyed in 1944 by the Germans as it was helping the RAF find their gun emplacements. Rebuilt since on the highest point of the peninsula, the column commemorates Sir John Doyle, Lieutenant-Governor of the Island from 1803 to 1813 and the man responsible for building the Island's three Martello Towers.

LIHOU

The smallest permanently inhabited island in the Channel Islands, Lihou lies off the western coast. At high tide its area is some 18 acres but, at low tide, it becomes joined to the mainland and can be reached on foot. When monks from Mont St Michel arrived on Lihou in 1114 they found dolmens and standing stones which suggest that this was a place of pagan worship. The monks used many of the stones in building their priory of Nôtre Dame de la Roche here. In 1415 Henry V seized all religious establishments belonging to French orders and gave the priory to Eton College, who held it until the Reformation. By 1660 the buildings were in ruins and little remains to be seen today.

The Island's name Lihou is derived from the Celtic word for mud. After the Second World War, Soay sheep, from Orkney, were introduced to the barren and windswept Island as they ate seaweed. Unfortunately the animals began to swim to the mainland and attack gardens.

Moulin Huet Bay

CHAPTER THREE
SARK & HERM

Transport on Sark

3
SARK & HERM

Introduction

Sark is, in fact, two islands: Great Sark and, very much smaller, Little Sark, which are linked by La Coupée, an isthmus. Though small, just 3 miles in length north to south and at most one and a half miles wide, Sark is a delightful island that is unlike any other. Like Jersey and Guernsey, Sark has its own parliament, the Chief Pleas, which is headed by the Seigneur. Still a feudal community, it is only the Seigneur who can own a bitch and keep pigeons on the Island and his permission must be sought before leases of property can be bought or sold.

The Island was permanently settled in Elizabethan times and the 40 tenements (or holdings) into which Sark was divided still remain today. Each tenement had a portion of the fertile inland plateau and also a piece of marginal cliff-top land. The 40 tenents were equipped to defend the Island and each was granted a seat in the Chief Pleas. Little has changed today, save for the muskets that they were given in the 16th century to defend their land, and the largest holding, in the middle of Great Sark, is still the home of the Seigneur and his property retains its original name of Le Manoir.

Sark is also famous as being the Island without motor vehicles (except for farm tractors) and aircraft flying under 500 feet are also banned unless it be a helicopter on a mercy mission. No exceptions are made to this though during the making of the television serial *Mr Pie* the film crew were allowed to bring a small saloon car to the Island on which the camera was mounted. However, in order to abide by the terms of the permission granted, the engine was removed from the car and it was drawn along by a horse. In fact, horses dominate life on the Island much as they did all over Great Britain in the last century.

La Seigneurie

With a landscape that has changed little in the last 100 years and with a magnificent coastline, Sark is the gem of the Channel. The Island's population of 550 is temporarily swelled to 65,000 during the summer months, when tourists take many ferries from Jersey and Guernsey to spend a day, or longer, exploring this remarkable Island. It is worth remembering that Sark pubs are not open on Sundays and neither tractors nor horses and carriages are allowed on the roads except for essential agricultural work or for transport to and from church.

Around Sark

MASELINE HARBOUR

This is the main harbour for shipping from Guernsey and Jersey and is the landing point used by the frequent ferry services during the summer months. Built of concrete and completed in 1949, the harbour was opened by HRH the Duke of Edinburgh during the Queen's visit to Sark.

From the harbour visitors' baggage is carried up the steep harbour hill on flat-bedded wagons pulled by tractors and the tourists have the choice of a stiff and often dusty walk to the village or a rather uncomfortable cart ride.

CREUX HARBOUR

Just to the south of Maseline Harbour, in the next bay, is this much more attractive harbour than its busy neighbour and it is used by local boats and visiting yachts. Created by blasting a tunnel through a rock wall into Baie de la Motte in 1563, with the breakwater being built in 1588, Creux Harbour is reputed to be the smallest harbour in the world.

THE AVENUE

The Avenue is Sark's main street and it is known locally as the M1. Two banks, the Midland and the Natwest guard one end of the street and the Island's post office can be found at the other. In between there is a whole host of shops and stores offering all the essentials as well as a host of souvenir items. Just off The Avenue, is the charming **Church of St Peter**. Though architecturally unremarkable, inside the Church, which dates from 1820, there are some interesting and touching memorials. The church bells were cast from a cannon belonging to the now disbanded Sark Militia.

Close by is **Island Hall** the main entertainment centre of the island. The Hall's neighbour is a small stone school which doubles as Sark's 'House of Parliament'. Here are held the quarterly meetings of Chief Pleas to which islanders and visitors are admitted. When the Pleas, and also the court sessions, are being held the children have the day off school.

As well as having, arguably, the world's smallest harbour, Sark also claims to have the world's smallest prison. Built in 1856 and of a rather peculiar design, the **Prison** serves Sark's needs as it is only used for short-term offenders; more serious criminals are sent to Guernsey for trial and punishment.

Like its larger neighbours, Sark was occupied by the Germans during the Second World War though many of the islanders evacuated before the invasion. The **German Occupation Museum** has a fascinating collection of relics from those days and, though some islanders were deported to Germany, life was comparatively easy on Sark as food was rather more plentiful and no fortifications were built here.

DIXCART BAY

The approach to Dixcart Bay, on the southern coast of the island, lies through the lovely, densely wooded **Dixcart Valley**. With a fine natural arch, impressive cliffs and safe bathing, the Bay is one of the most frequented on the Island. To the left of the Bay, on the headland of **Pointe Château**, there once stood a small French fort. Built by the French during their occupation of Sark in 1549, all that now remains to interest the visitor is a cannon embedded in the ground.

Dixcart is Sark's oldest hotel. Once a 16th century feudal farm longhouse, it lies high up in a sun-trapped valley yet within easy walking distance of the village. Enjoying a secluded world of its own, the property encompasses an extensive acreage of medieval hand-terraced gardens, cliff paths through the densely wooded Dixcart Valley, and the sheltered Bay of Dixcart. This historic Bay is on the Hotel's own land and within five minutes descent from its gardens. Safe for swimming Dixcart Bay provides a sheltered anchorage for visiting yachtsmen of every nationality. Since its early existence, the Hotel has attracted Princes and Kings, writers and poets - including Victor Hugo and Swinburn. All have loved

Sark's unique stillness, serenity and gentle hospitality.

Dixcart is without doubt a charming hotel. It is family owned and managed and has the mellow ambience of its ancient stone walls and unique rural surrounding - a place, one might think, where time stands still. A look into the bedrooms reveals a style of furnishing and decor totally suited to this period building, carefully and tastefully applied. All the bedrooms are en-suite and centrally heated. There are three comfortable lounges, one with a residents' bar and two with original stone fireplaces intact, affording ample room for relaxation.

The candlelit restaurant overlooks the gardens and offers good and reasonably priced food and wines, whilst in the separate, fully licensed Dixcart Inn, snacks are served and children are welcome. AA and Egon Ronay recommended, Dixcart is featured in most major guides. Sark, free of cars and motorbikes, is a romantic and dream island and the Dixcart is the perfect setting in which to enjoy it and perhaps fulfil your own dreams.

The Dixcart Hotel, Dixcart Bay Tel: 01481 832015
Fax: 01481 832164

HOG'S BACK

This aptly named ridge separates the bays of Derrible and Dixcart.

LA FREGONDÉE

This little hamlet is reached by a track and it overlooks the Gouliot Passage between Sark and Brecqhou. Before the thatched roofs of the cottages were replaced with corrugated metal the hamlet was much prettier but, like most buildings on Sark, the thatch was replaced because of the fire hazard it presented.

GOULIOT HEADLAND

On the west coast of Sark, the headland overlooks the island of Brecqhou across the narrow Gouliot Passage. The **Gouliot Caves**, tunnelled into the headland, are fantastically studded with sea anemones of various colours. The first cave, curiously named the Chinmey, leads to a great cavern which resembles a huge church. For those who wish to explore them remember to take a torch and also be aware that the caves become cut off at high tide.

Once used as a port, **Havre Gosselin**, to the south of the headland, is only used today when weather conditions on the eastern coast of Sark are unsuitable. Before the quay and steps were built here in 1912, the only landing place was via an iron ladder rising from the deep water to the cliff path. Sloping slightly outwards the climb, particularly from a small boat tossing on the waves, must have been very daunting. The ladder can still be seen but, today, passengers are taken from the ships by small boats. From this bay, on a stormy night in 1868, Jeremiah Pilcher and four companions attempted to cross to Guernsey in a small boat. All lost their lives and Jeremiah's body was eventually found washed up on the Isle of Wight. The stone obelisk of the **Pilcher Monument**, which stands on the cliffs to the south of Havre Gosselin, commemorates the tragedy.

Victor Hugo Cave, at the end of Longue Pointe to the south of Havre Gosselin, was given this name after the poet visited the island and is best reached by boat.

Falle's Beau Regard Camp Site offer idyllic camping on the spectacular west coast on a small, select, sheltered site with panoramic views and unparalleled sunsets. The site offers good facilities including showers and well-stocked village shops are but ten minutes walk away. A comprehensive brochure is available for this very select and limited Camp site and early booking is essential. Open March to September.

Call in and enjoy the hospitality of Stan and Christine Falle in the old 16th century **Falle's Barn Bar**. Originally a farm barn forming one of the first tenements on the Island, it is fully licensed and offers home-made sloe gin, local beers and proprietary brands. Inexpensive bar lunches, snacks and evening meals are served throughout the season. There's a sunny sheltered garden where you can enjoy soft drinks and ices, teas and coffee.

Falle's Barn Bar and Camp Site, Beau Regard Tel: 01481 832186

LA SEIGNEURIE

This is the ancestral home of the Seigneur of Sark and it began life as la Perronerie, the home of one of the original tenants who came here in 1565 with Helier de Carteret. Built on the site of the old priory of St Magloire, which was founded in the 6th century, the oldest part of the present house dates from 1565 but the main body of the building was erected in 1730 by Dame Suzanne Le Pelley, the first ruler of the Island to live in the house. Though the house is never open to the public, the gardens can be seen Monday to Friday, Easter to October and also on Saturdays during July and August. Here the attractions include a fine flower display, with many sub-tropical specimens, the Island's only dove-cote and a saker (a type of cannon) which came from the Tower of London and was given to Sark by Elizabeth I.

PORT DU MOULIN

The name of the bay makes reference to a watermill which once stood here. Belonging to the monastery of St Magloire, the watermill was probably the first to be built in the Channel Islands.

The Window in the Rock, a small aperture in cliff face here, was made in the 19th century to enable the Seigneur's men to haul vraic (seaweed) up from the beach to be used as fertiliser. Now a dramatic viewpoint, the drop to the sea from here is sheer.

From here it is possible, at low tide, to walk through a natural archway and out to **Les Autelets**. These huge rocks with flat tops are known by the French word for little altars and they are the home of thousands of kittiwakes.

BOUTIQUES CAVES

Second only to the caves at Les Gouliots in size and interest these caves are best explored during the Spring low tides and are light enough to make a torch unnecessary. It is said that the name means stores or shops and came about when the caves were used by smugglers. This, however, is unlikely as freetrading was legal in the Channel Islands and so there was no need to smuggle goods.

L'EPERQUERIE COMMON

Situated on the northern tip of Sark, this wild area has a network of footpaths through the gorse and heather. The name, L'Eperquerie, is derived from the French word perques (poles) which were used for drying fish. An the eastern shore is the Island's original landing and above it stands an upturned cannon that came from the East Indiaman Valentine that was wrecked off Bercqhou in 1781.

LES FONTAINES BAY

Named the Fairy Grotto by a local artist, William Toplis, it is possible, when standing in the correct position, to look through two natural arches and see the shape of a lady (the Fairy).

GULL'S CHAPEL

Situated at **Grève de la Ville**, on the east coast of Sark, down steep cliffs is La Chapelle des Mauvres (The Gull's Chapel). This, however, is not a place of worship but an arched rock that is shaped like a chapel. Its name is thus self-explanatory.

POINT ROBERT LIGHTHOUSE

Situated half way down the cliff, on the east coast, and reached by a flight of steps, the Lighthouse is open to visitors in the afternoon.

Situated on the east of the Island near to Point Robert Lighthouse and Grève de la Ville Bay, you'll find **The Mermaid Tavern**, easily accessed from the village and the harbour. It was built in 1928 and has been owned by the same family ever since. Extensions were built in 1968 to include the present function room, where discos are held twice weekly throughout the summer to raise funds for the St John Ambulance Marine ambulance, Flying Christine 111. A pool table, juke box, Shove Ha'penny and pin table amusements are very popular and are available and in use year-round. Light snacks, coffee and tea are served daily (except Sundays) from 10 am until 11 pm or 11.45 pm on disco nights.

The Mermaid Tavern Tel: 01481 832022

LA COUPÉE

This narrow isthmus which joins Great Sark to Little Sark makes a spectacular walk with a drop of around 260 feet on each side. To the east the drop is sheer all the way down to the sea but, on the western side, the drop down to Grande Grève Bay is more gentle. Until 1900, La Coupée was crumbling and unprotected from the elements and very hazardous to cross. Attempts were made to make the crossing safer but it was not until 1945, with the help of German prisoners-of-war, that the concrete road was constructed by the Occupying force. The railings, still there today, were installed by British troops after the liberation of the Island.

LITTLE SARK

Less crowded than Great Sark, Little Sark has plenty to offer the visitor including a superb coastline. On the east coast is **Pot Bay**, so called because of the cauldron-shaped cavity found here in the cliffs.

On the south coast, is a much loved beauty spot, **Venus Pool**. This sheltered rock pool is deep and an excellent place for divers.

On the west coast, at **Port Gorey**, are the **Silver Mines**. Lying directly west of Pot Bay, they are situated on the other end of the rich mineral vein that contains silver, lead and copper. Mining started here in around 1835 and carried on for 10 years. Though the mining activity was extensive the Silver Mines were never economic and following a number of disasters they were closed. Most of the mineshafts were filled in but their positions and those of the ventilation chimneys are still clearly visible.

BRECQHOU

This small Island lies to the west of Great Sark, opposite Gouliot Headland. Just half a mile from east to west and slightly shorter north to south, this is a flat, windswept land that not easily accessible. There are two landing places on the island which is surrounded by high cliffs and these are only usable during calm weather. One of the tenements of Sark, Brecqhou has a farm, a mansion and a helicopter pad.

Around Herm

The Island is, geographically, a mini Guernsey, and it lies just three miles across the Little Russel passage from its large neighbour. Some one and a half miles from north to south and just half a mile wide, the high land lies to the south, whilst the northern third of Herm, known as the Common, is a low-lying plain of sand dunes.

Herm's name does not come from the dwelling place of a hermit, as might be supposed, but it is said to mean deserted or uncultivated land. In the 16th and 17th centuries it was used as a hunting ground for the governors of Guernsey who came here to shoot deer and rabbits. The rabbits still abound particularly on the Common as they have no natural predator and they keep the turf here short allowing such minute plants as the saxifrage to thrive.

This plain dune area is also home to a number of prehistoric remains. The largest and best preserved of the neolithic burial chambers is **Robert's Cross** and other fragments can be found on **Le Petit Monceau** and **Le Grand Monceau**, the two hillocks rising up from the Common.

La Pierre aux Rats, a stone obelisk overlooking north beach which acts as a seamark, was built by quarrymen to replace the original monolith they destroyed when extracting granite. Herm was once famous for its granite; with a reputation for being hard wearing it was extracted and exported to England. The industry flourished here in the first half of the 19th century and three large quarries were dug into the hillside facing Guernsey. Both the harbour and the village clustered around it owe their existence to the industry.

Overlooking the harbour is **St Tugual's Chapel**, the origin of which is uncertain though it is undoubtedly ancient. Possibly dating back to the 6th century and built by St Magloire around the time he founded a religious house on Sark, the chapel was certainly here in 1186 as it was mentioned in a Bull of Pope Urban III. Until 1881, monks have inhabited Herm on and off and the Chapel has always been in use though not always as a place of worship. Restored in 1913, some excellent stained glass windows were more recently installed and the Chapel is once again being used for services on Sundays.

The manor house, **Le Manoir**, was extended and altered to its present form, with battlements and machicolatons, by Blücher von Wahlstatt, a German prince who leased the Island at the turn of the century. The Prince also laid the metalled road up the hill and planted groves of pine and evergreen oak on the island's summit. The small fairy-tale tower behind the manor house was converted from an old mill.

JETHOU

Lying to the southwest of Herm, the Island is only some 600 yards in diameter and is in private hands. Though smaller that its neighbour, Jethou is slightly higher than Herm and the slope facing it across the Percée Passage is, in spring, carpeted by bluebells which give it the name **Fairy Wood**. Among the tenants of this Crown property was novelist Compton Mackenzie, who based *Fairy Gold* in Herm and Jethou.

La Coupée

CHAPTER FOUR ALDERNEY

Braye Harbour

4
ALDERNEY

Introduction

The third largest of the Channel Islands, Alderney lies in the Bay of St Malo just 8 miles from mainland France. Three and half miles long by at most one and half miles wide, this most northerly of the Channel Islands holds a strategic position at the entrance to the English Channel

With a strong character and identity all its own, Alderney is charming and its variety of habitats support a wide range of wild life. With heathland, cliffs, rocky shorelines, open fields, wooded valleys and sandy beaches the Island is a home or refuge to some 200 different species of bird. Also playing an important part in the natural life of the Island is the wild rabbit. Off-shore seals, dolphins and porpoises can sometimes be seen playing whilst the large expanse of rockpools reveal, at low tide, a myriad of marine life.

Around Alderney

ST ANNE

The Island's capital and only town, the majority of the population live here. Originally a group of medieval farmsteads built around the Marais Square area, the narrow cobbled streets, the many whitewashed stone houses and the welcoming hostelries make this a very friendly place to visit. The town was enlarged, first in the 18th century using the wealth gained from privateering and then again in the 19th century when labour was imported to build the harbour and fortifications.

The town's main road, **Victoria Street**, is full of elegant small shops; no supermarkets and multiple stores here. Before Queen Victoria's visit, in

St Anne's Church

1854, it was called Rue Grosnez and half way along stands the Albert Memorial which commemorates this first royal visit to the island.

At the northern end of the street is **The Butes**. The name means archery ground and this was probably the land where the militiamen practised their bow skills. Today it is a pleasant green and the home of the Alderney Cricket Club. One of the Island's most famous inhabitants John Arlott, who retired here in 1981 after becoming a household name for his cricket commentaries for the BBC, was a past president of the Club and he is responsible for introducing Ian Botham to the delights of Alderney. Sadly missed by the Island since his death 1991, Arlott was also a wine buff whose cellar of excellent wine was legendary. He is buried in St Anne's churchyard.

Built by Sir Giles Gilbert Scott and completed in 1850, **St Anne's Church** is probably the best church in the Channel Islands. Its handsome tower is a landmark and most striking of all is the stone from which it was built as Caen stone was used unlike most Channel Island churches which made do with local stone. Much has been done to restore the Church to its former glory in the days before the German Occupation and the bells have been recovered from France where the Germans sent them to be melted down for munitions.

As well as being the building where the court sits and the States have their assembly, the **Court House**, built in 1850, has exhibitions that are of historical interest. The assembly chamber has been fully restored after it was misused by the Germans and visitors are welcome to sit in on meetings of the States, though, of course, only to observe.

Opened in 1972, **Alderney Society's Museum** is housed in the Ssland's old school building which dates from 1790. The collections range from the time of the Neolithic settlers through the centuries to the years of the German Occupation. In an extension opened in 1984, can also be seen the crafts and trades of the Island along with its natural history and the latest of Alderney's stamps.

"Family owned and family run", that's the proud claim of Steve and Pauline, the proprietors of The **Belle Vue Hotels**. For more than 21 years they have, with their professional, efficient business approach, created a warm and friendly environment into which they have welcomed thousands of visitors and introduced them to Alderney. The two adjacent hotels form a complex which is the largest and probably the busiest in the

Island. The main Hotel overlooks the harbour and Braye beach and is only a very short walk from the centre of St Anne. There are 27 en-suite bedrooms equipped with satellite television, radio, tea and coffee makers, direct dial telephone and central heating. Two special mini suites are available at no extra cost for non-smokers.

Belle Vue Hotels

Granny's is the Hotel restaurant where both à la carte and table d'hôte menus are available. Everything is home-made and the best fresh local produce is used whenever possible. Food is available all day in the Hotel where bar snacks can be ordered at lunchtime and the coffee shop is open daily from 10 am until 5 pm serving sandwiches, great cakes and cappuccino coffee. Afternoon teas are another speciality and the garden allows for al fresco meals and drinks at lunchtime or evenings.

The Belle Vue Hotels are open all year and are ideal for holidays, short breaks or even weekends away. Inclusive holiday packages are available including flights, offering definite savings. Ask for an information pack.

There are no single supplements and children from 2 to 11 years have a 50% reduction when sharing with parents.

Belle Vue Hotels, Alderney Tel: 01481 822844
Fax: 01481 823601

THE SECOND WORLD WAR IN ALDERNEY

When it became increasingly likely that an invasion by the Germans of the Channel Islands, and particularly Alderney, would take place the Island was evacuated by its inhabitants with Guernsey rescue parties evacuating the livestock and useful stores. By the time the Germans arrived, on July 2nd 1940, Alderney was deserted save for seven islanders.

Its strategic importance, that had shaped its landscape over the centuries, was, probably, the chief reason for the invasion and also, of course, its British sovereignty. By October 1941, the Germans had turned the whole Island, once again, into a fortress. Several thousands slave labourers were brought in from occupied Europe to carry out the work and, as there were no civilians to witness the manner in which they were treated, their sufferings were much harsher than those administered on the larger islands. The Germans also had a concentration camp here, built in 1943, and under the control of the infamous SS. With neither a gas chamber nor a crematorium, the Germans transformed a tunnel into which the prisoners were to be walled in if the Island was invade by allied forces.

As well as re-fortifying the old forts thousands of mines were laid on the beaches, the great anti-tank wall was built at Longis Bay and bunkers appeared everywhere. Many of the structures remain to this day and the exploitation of Alderney extended to desecrating St Anne's Church, destroying dwellings and uprooting boundaries. During 1942, British troops carried out two raids; one on Burhou and, the second, a reconnaissance landing on Les Casquets lighthouse where the occupying Germans were taken prisoner.

The German garrison on the Island finally surrendered on 16th May 1945, a week after the liberation of Jersey and Guernsey. Then followed a period of rehabilitation and rebuilding before the first islanders returned to Alderney in December 1945. The full truth about the occupation of Alderney will probably never been known as there was no one to see. The Hammond Memorial, dedicated in October 1966, was provided by the Hammond family in memory of all those who suffered on the Island during the Second World War.

BRAYE HARBOUR

Today, the old harbour is full of character with 18th century houses, old warehouses and yards and the Sailing Club's headquarters are also here. The Commercial quay dates from the turn of this century and the Germans built an extension but this fell into disrepair and was demolished in 1981. This harbour also had one particular disadvantage in that it dried out at low tide and so the new harbour was built which, unfortunately, lacks the charm of its older neighbour. The Old Jetty and Douglas Quay are no longer used by shipping but are popular with swimmers and sunbathers.

Some 400 years ago an Elizabethan warship was shipwrecked off the coast of Braye and she still lies some 90 feet below waves half a mile off shore. Early exploration or the wreck brought up several items of interest to shore and visitors can view some of the shipboard material, weapons and artefacts at Alderney Museum and at the Shed in Braye Harbour (open in the afternoon in the summer). Unfortunately, full recovery of the wreck is prohibitively expensive.

Alderney is unique among the Channel Islands in that it still retains its railway, now run by the **Alderney Railway Society**. Opened in 1980, the Society, who are all volunteers, run trains between Braye Station and Mannez Quarry some 2 miles away. The two London Underground carriages, that comprise the present railway stock, are pulled by either of the two diesel locomotives or by one of the small petrol driven railcars. As well as running the line, the volunteers also man the stations and during the season there is a regular service on Wednesday, Saturday and Sunday afternoons. The service runs daily during Alderney Week.

Alderney is a particularly beautiful and unspoiled island, offering superb beaches with safe bathing. Located on one of Alderney's finest beaches - Braye Bay, is the **Sea View Hotel** where guests can literally step out of the hotel onto its sandy shore. The buildings were originally a dockside inn, shops and cellar stores off the old Douglas Quay Harbour and built about 1750. After being partially destroyed, the Hotel was rebuilt in 1949, since when it has undergone major alterations and now offers much improved facilities. Above all, this is a family hotel with a friendly and helpful team looking after your needs. The accommodation is light and airy with en-suite facilities in all bedrooms. Most have a sea view and all rooms have colour television, telephone, hospitality tray and central heating. From the very popular Lounge Bar and Fisherman's Bar you can sit and enjoy the views of the harbour and beach whist enjoying a refreshing drink or bar snack. The Restaurant in the old quay cellars offers an extensive menu with fresh local seafood being a speciality and you can choose from a varied range of wines to accompany your meal. There are many activities available at the Sea View but most of all you'll enjoy the hotel service, atmosphere and superb location. Open throughout the year.

Sea View Hotel, Braye Harbour Tel: 01481 822738
Fax: 01481 823572

Of great necessity to many people and families visiting the Island is - a car; ensuring you have the least trouble getting up and down from the beaches, for exploring, and affording you the freedom to stop when and wherever you choose. **Braye Hire Cars** therefore fulfils a vital need on the Island and the owners Nigel and June offer a professional and friendly service to many visitors throughout the year.

Braye Hire Cars

Mouriaux Garage had been in existence for 24 years when Nigel and June became the new owners six years ago and, although the garage is still operating, this family run business now provides the car rental requirements of Alderney. June will meet you at the airport or harbour or even deliver you to your hotel. She is a fund of information and is happy to answer all your questions as well as providing you with a map of the Island. Open times are 8 am until 5.30 pm but the business can be contacted until 9 pm. Don't forget - it's a good idea to book ahead to save disappointment.

Braye Hire Cars, Mouriax Garage, Carriere Viront
Tel: 01481 823881 Fax: 01481 824043

FORT ALBERT

Situated on Mont Touraille and overlooking the harbour and Braye Bay, this is the chief fort of Alderney. The Fort's arsenal lies at the foot of the hill along with Mount Hale Battery and the former garrison football pitch. An unusual covered way, in granite, runs from the Arsenal to the entrance of the Fort. Fort Albert, named after Queen Victoria's husband, is now derelict and not open to the public.

CORBLETS BAY

With its safe bathing and excellent surf, Corblets Bay is one of the favoured bay's on Alderney. It is also dominated by **Fort Corblets**, now a handsome private residence which retains a martial air though traces of additions made by the Germans are barely visible. Built in 1855, the Fort was originally mounted with 13 guns and provided accommodation for around 60 officers and men.

MANNEZ GARENNE

Occupying the northeast tip of the Island, Mannez Garenne is an area of grassland from which the sandstone that was used in the construction of the breakwater at Braye was quarried. On the rocky and inhospitable coast here was built **Quesnard Lighthouse** in 1912. The Lighthouse is open to visitors in the afternoon and there are spectacular views from its lantern.

LONGIS BAY

One of the best walks on Alderney can be taken along the stretch of coastline between Mannez Lighthouse and the Bay. The wild and rocky coastline gives way to the quiet sands in the bay which are popular with residents and visitors as the German Anti-tank wall shelters the beach. From here, at low tide, **Raz Island** can be reached along a causeway. With old and new defences, an art gallery and a collection of stuffed birds it is well worth the walk.

At the southern end of the bay is the **Nunnery**, an ancient fort that is probably of Roman origin. It got its unusual name because the garrison stationed here found it so lonely!

LONGIS COMMON

Traces of quarrying can be found along with a few houses and some German defences on the Common inland from the Bay. An Iron Age site was discovered here, in 1968, when the golf course was being laid out and the pots that were found can be seen in the Museum.

The Devereux House Hotel

Situated in a lush, sheltered valley, only 100 yards from the 9-hole golf course and five minutes walk to one of Alderney's principle beaches at Longis, **The Devereux House Hotel** is ideally situated for activity or quiet leisurely holiday breaks. The Devereux, designed as a country residence in the grand style, is a friendly hotel with good food and hospitality to match. Most rooms are en-suite and all have tea and coffee making facilities and TV. There is a licensed bar with lunches available daily and a very pleasant restaurant where superb cuisine, prepared by the hotel chefs, is served in comfort and style.

For something completely different and exciting, take a trial flight in a light aircraft around the islands and to Northern France, or learn to fly in 2/3 weeks, with the sister company to the Hotel - Stratair. From the Hotel, guests are well placed to take advantage of the many activities available, including fishing, wind surfing, horse riding, tennis, clay pigeon shooting and cycling. Golf clubs and fishing rods can be hired from the hotel. Flight inclusive holidays are available at greatly reduced prices.

The Devereux House Hotel, Val Fontaine
Tel & Fax: 01481 822549

HANGING ROCKS

On the east coast, are the Hanging Rocks, two rocks, one larger than the other, that lean like the Tower of Pisa. Legend has it that, many years ago, Jerseymen, keen to acquire Alderney for themselves, secured a rope from one of the rocks to their boat and tried to tow the Island away. As they rowed away so the rock began to lean. A similar story tells of how Guernseymen tried to capture the Island the same way.

Known locally as Madame Robilliard's Nose, one further local story would have visitors believe that this is in fact the unfortunate woman's nose. Caught prying into the affairs of a wizard, the fellow cast a spell upon the woman which caused her nose to grow to an enormous size. Removed by an exorcist, the wizard acquired the nose and placed it as a warning to other nosy people. Many more stories local stories abound regarding these amazing rocks, each more elaborate than the last.

TELEGRAPH BAY

As well as the remains of telegraph cable visitors to the bay can explore a fine cave here at low tide. Bathing here is excellent but be warned though because at high tide the base of the cliffs are inaccessible.

On top of the cliffs is **Telegraph Tower**, from which the Bay got its name as the Tower was used in the early 19th century for signalling to the other islands. Now closed to the public, a trip up to the cliff tops is well worth the effort because from here, near a German look-out post, there are excellent views and, in clear weather, all the Channel Islands can be seen.

LA GIFFOINE

This broad expanse of heathland, between the clifftops and the arable land near Braye, was once the site of a beacon and is also where a massive German defence stood.

FORT CLONQUE

Reached by a causeway at anytime other than high tide, this Victorian fort was built to defend the Swinge. A particularly romantic fellow, the Fort's architect, Captain William Jervois, included many elaborate additions to his buildings that did not have any military purpose. The Fort is now owned by the Landmark Trust and has been restored and converted into holiday flats. Fort Clonque overlooks Hannaine Bay which is very suitable for bathing when sand is exposed.

On Alderney, especially on the Pointe de Clonque, there are bonfires on the first Sunday in Lent. Called Dimanche de Brandons, after dancing round the flames the young islanders would run back to St Anne with burning brands of straw.

Corblets Bay and Fort

TOURIST INFORMATION CENTRES

States of Jersey Tourism Office
Liberation Square, St Helier 01534 500888 / 500777

Guernsey Information Centre
North Esplanade, St peter Port 01481 723552

Sark Tourism
The Information Centre, Sark 01451 832345

Alderney Tourism
Information Centre, Victoria Street 01481 823737

INDEX

The Hidden Places Series

ORDER FORM

To order more copies of this title or any of the others in this series please complete the order form below and send to:

Travel Publishing Ltd.
7a Apollo House, Calleva Park, Aldermaston, Berks RG7 8TN

Title	Price	Quantity	Value
Channel Islands	£6.99	....	....
Devon & Cornwall	£4.95	....	....
Dorset, Hants & Isle of Wight	£4.95	....	....
East Anglia	£4.95	....	....
Heart of England	£4.95	....	....
Lancashire & Cheshire	£4.95	....	....
North Wales	£4.95	....	....
Northumberland & Durham	£4.95	....	....
Somerset, Avon, Glocs & Wilts	£4.95	....	....
South East	£4.95	....	....
South Wales	£4.95	....	....
Thames & Chilterns	£5.99	....	....
Welsh Borders	£5.99	....	....
Yorkshire & Humberside	£4.95	....	....
England	£8.99	....	....
Ireland	£8.99	....	....
Scotland	£8.99	....	....
Wales	£8.99	....	....
	TOTAL	______	______

For orders of less than 10 copies please add £1 per book for postage & packing. Orders over 10 copies P & P free.

I enclose a cheque for £ .... made payable to Travel Publishing Ltd

NAME ....

ADDRESS ....

....

POSTCODE ....

Plate 1

JERSEY

ALDERNEY

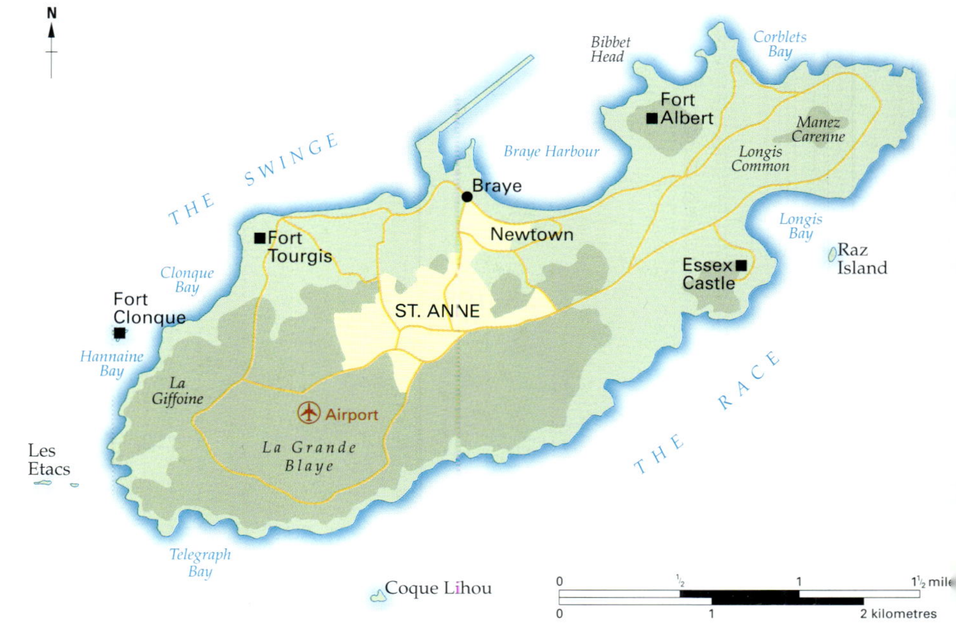

Plate 2

GUERNSEY

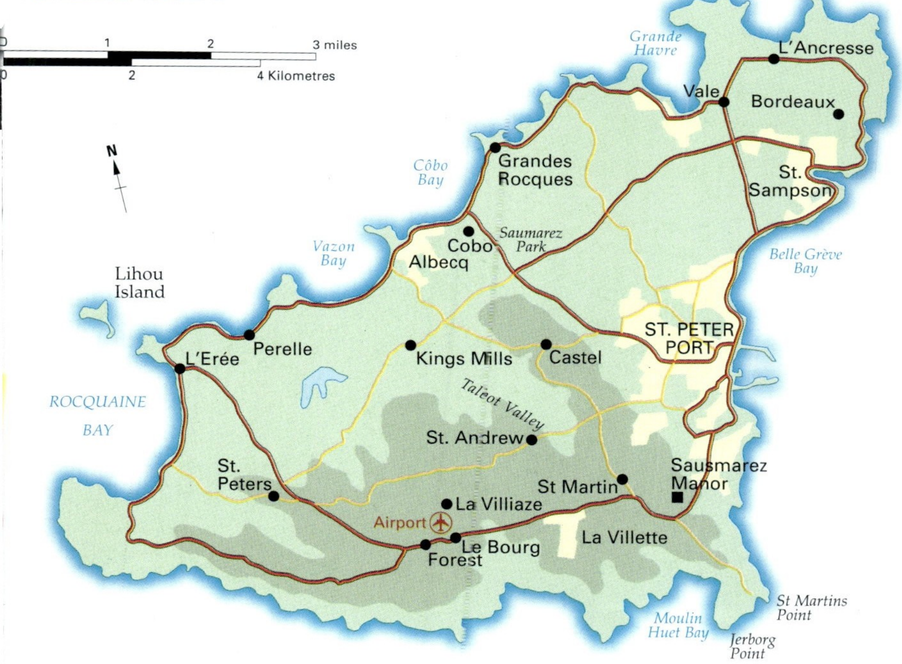

HERM

SARK